U0453738

麦格希 中英双语阅读文库

世界上最伟大的声音

第2辑

【美】 弗里德 (Freed, K.) ●主编

刘慧●译

麦格希中英双语阅读文库编委会●编

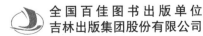

全国百佳图书出版单位

吉林出版集团股份有限公司

图书在版编目（CIP）数据

世界上最伟大的声音. 第2辑 / (美) 弗里德
(Freed, K.) 主编；刘慧译；麦格希中英双语阅读文库编
委会编. -- 2版. -- 长春：吉林出版集团股份有限公司,
2018.3（2022.1重印）
　（麦格希中英双语阅读文库）
　ISBN 978-7-5581-4788-3

　Ⅰ.①世… Ⅱ.①弗… ②刘… ③麦… Ⅲ.①英语—
汉语—对照读物②演讲—世界—选集 Ⅳ.①H319.4：I

中国版本图书馆CIP数据核字(2018)第046436号

世界上最伟大的声音　第2辑

编：	麦格希中英双语阅读文库编委会
插　画：	齐　航　李延霞
责任编辑：	沈丽娟
封面设计：	冯冯翼
开　本：	660mm × 960mm　1/16
字　数：	209千字
印　张：	9.25
版　次：	2018年3月第2版
印　次：	2022年1月第2次印刷

出　版：	吉林出版集团股份有限公司
发　行：	吉林出版集团外语教育有限公司
地　址：	长春市福祉大路5788号龙腾国际大厦B座7层
电　话：	总编办：0431-81629929
	发行部：0431-81629927　0431-81629921(Fax)
印　刷：	北京一鑫印务有限责任公司

ISBN 978-7-5581-4788-3　定价：35.00元

前言 *PREFACE*

英国思想家培根说过：阅读使人深刻。阅读的真正目的是获取信息，开拓视野和陶冶情操。从语言学习的角度来说，学习语言若没有大量阅读就如隔靴搔痒，因为阅读中的语言是最丰富、最灵活、最具表现力、最符合生活情景的，同时读物中的情节、故事引人入胜，进而能充分调动读者的阅读兴趣，培养读者的文学修养，至此，语言的学习水到渠成。

"麦格希中英双语阅读文库"在世界范围内选材，涉及科普、社会文化、文学名著、传奇故事、成长励志等多个系列，充分满足英语学习者课外阅读之所需，在阅读中学习英语、提高能力。

◎难度适中

本套图书充分照顾读者的英语学习阶段和水平，从读者的阅读兴趣出发，以难易适中的英语语言为立足点，选材精心、编排合理。

◎精品荟萃

本套图书注重经典阅读与实用阅读并举。既包含国内外脍炙人口、耳熟能详的美文，又包含科普、人文、故事、励志类等多学科的精彩文章。

◎功能实用

本套图书充分体现了双语阅读的功能和优势，充分考虑到读者课外阅读的方便，超出核心词表的词汇均出现在使其意义明显的语境之中，并标注释义。

鉴于编者水平有限，凡不周之处，谬误之处，皆欢迎批评教正。

我们真心地希望本套图书承载的文化知识和英语阅读的策略对提高读者的英语著作欣赏水平和英语运用能力有所裨益。

丛书编委会

Contents

Three Stories from My Life I
我人生中的三个故事 I / 1

Three Stories from My Life II
我人生中的三个故事 II / 7

Three Stories from My Life III
我人生中的三个故事 III / 12

Hard Work and Determination Pays Off
(Excerpt)
努力工作，决战人生（节选）/ 17

Unleashing Your Creativity
释放你的创造力 / 21

First Inaugural Address (Excerpt)
就职演讲（节选）/ 26

Remarks in Shanghai Meeting with Future
Chinese Leaders(Excerpt)
上海会见青年学生的演讲（节选）/ 30

The Fringe Benefits of Failure, and the Importance of
Imagination I
失败的好处和想象力的重要性 I / 34

The Fringe Benefits of Failure, and the Importance of Imagination II
失败的好处和想象力的重要性 II / 39

The Fringe Benefits of Failure, and the Importance of Imagination III
失败的好处和想象力的重要性 III / 44

Message of Hope(Excerpt)
播撒希望（节选）/ 50

Beautiful Smile and Love(Excerpt)
美丽的微笑和爱（节选）/ 53

Concession Speech I(Excerpt)
退选演讲 I（节选）/ 58

Concession Speech II(Excerpt)
退选演讲 II（节选）/ 62

Concession Speech III(Excerpt)
退选演讲 III（节选）/ 66

Nobel Prize Acceptance Speech
诺贝尔文学奖获奖演说 / 71

Unite to Create Prosperous Tomorrow
联合起来，共创美好未来 / 75

First Inaugural Address(Excerpt)
第一次就职演说（节选）/ 79

Harvard Commencement Address I(Excerpt)
哈佛毕业典礼演讲Ⅰ（节选）/ 83

Harvard Commencement Address II(Excerpt)
哈佛毕业典礼演讲II（节选）/ 87

Speaks at Tsinghua University I(Excerpt)
清华大学演讲Ⅰ（节选）/ 91

Speaks at Tsinghua University II(Excerpt)
清华大学演讲II（节选）/ 95

Inequity and Complexity of the Word I(Excerpt)
世界之不平等与复杂性Ⅰ（节选）/ 99

Inequity and Complexity of the Word II(Excerpt)
世界之不平等与复杂性II（节选）/ 105

Commencement Address at Harvard University(Excerpt)
哈佛大学毕业典礼上的演讲（节选）/ 109

Address at the Democratic National Convention I
民主党大会上的演讲 I / 113

Address at the Democratic National Convention II
民主党大会上的演讲 II / 117

Address at the Democratic National
Convention III
民主党大会上的演讲 III / 121

We Are What We Choose I
决定成就我们 I / 126

We Are What We Choose II
决定成就我们 II / 131

Commencement Address in Yale University
在耶鲁大学毕业典礼上的演讲 / 136

Three Stories from My Life I

Steve Jobs Stanford University Commencement Address, 2005

The first story is about connecting the dots.

I dropped out of Reed College after the first six months, but then stayed around as a *drop-in* for another 18 months or so before I really quit. So why did I *drop out*?

It started before I was born. My

我人生中的三个故事 I

史蒂夫·乔布斯 2005 年在斯坦福大学毕业典礼上的演讲

第一个故事是关于如何把人生中的点点滴滴串联在一起的。

我在里德学院学习了6个月后就休学了，后返回学校又继续学习了18个月，然后就彻底退学了。那么，我为什么休学呢？

这得从我出生前讲起。我的亲生母亲当时还在读研究生，是个年轻

---

drop-in *n.* 顺便（或偶然）拜访   drop out 退出；退学

biological mother was a young, *unwed* graduate student, and she decided to put me up for adoption. She felt very strongly that I should be adopted by college graduates, so everything was all set for me to be adopted at birth by a lawyer and his wife—except that when I popped out they decided at the last minute that they really wanted a girl. So my parents, who were on a waiting list, got a call in the middle of the night asking, "We've got an unexpected baby boy; do you want him?" They said, "Of course." My biological mother found out later that my mother had never graduated from college and that my father had never graduated from high school. She refused to sign the final adoption papers. She only *relented* a few months later when my parents promised that I would go to college.

的未婚妈妈，因此她决定让别人收养我。她坚定地认为领养我的人应该接受过大学教育，所以，她就准备让一对律师夫妇收养我。但是没有料到的是，当我出生之后这对夫妇却在最后一刻反悔了，因为他们想收养一个女孩。这样，候补名单上的一对夫妇，也就是我后来的养父母，在一天半夜里接到这样一通电话："我们这有一名意外出生的男婴，你们要领养他吗？"他们的回答是："当然要。"后来，当我的生母得知我的养母未曾念过大学，而我的养父则连高中都没读完后，她拒绝在领养文件上做最后签字。几个月后，我的养父母保证将来一定会让我上大学后，她的态度才得以缓和。我的人生也就此拉开了序幕。

---

unwed *adj.* 未婚的   relent *v.* 变宽厚；变温和；心软

This was the start in my life.

And 17 years later I did go to college. But I *naively* chose a college that was almost as expensive as Stanford, and all of my working-class parents' savings were being spent on my college tuition. After six months, I couldn't see the value in it. I had no idea what I wanted to do with my life and no idea how college was going to help me figure it out. And here I was spending all of the money my parents had saved their entire life. So I decided to drop out and trust that it would all work out okay. It was pretty scary at the time, but looking back it was one of the best decisions I ever made. The minute I dropped out I could stop taking the required classes that didn't interest me, and begin dropping in on the ones that looked far more

17年后，我考上了大学。但是，我却无知地选择了一所学费几乎跟斯坦福一样贵的大学，而我那工薪阶层的养父母将毕生积蓄都奉献给了我的学费。6个月后，我看不出学习这门专业的价值。而且那时，我并不清楚自己这辈子要干什么，也不知道上大学能对我有什么帮助，只知道为了让我读书，我父母花光了他们这辈子所有的积蓄。所以，我决定休学，我相信车到山前必有路，船到桥头自然直。在当时来看，这是个相当可怕的决定，可现在回想起来，它却是我这辈子做过的最明智的决定。从我休学的那刻开始，我就再也不用上那些我不感兴趣的必修课，而是把时间拿去

naively *adv.* 无邪地；天真烂漫地

interesting.

It wasn't all romantic. I didn't have a dorm room, so I slept on the floor in friends' rooms. I returned coke bottles for the five cent deposits to buy food with, and I would walk the seven miles across town every Sunday night to get one good meal a week at the Hare Krishna temple. I loved it. And much of what I *stumbled into* by following my curiosity and intuition turned out to be priceless later on. Let me give you one example:

Reed College at that time offered perhaps the best *calligraphy* instruction in the country. Throughout the campus every poster, every label on every drawer, was beautifully hand calligraphed. Because I had dropped out and didn't have to take the normal

---

听那些我喜欢的课。

这并不那么浪漫。我没有宿舍，所以只能睡在朋友房间的地板上，用回收一个空可乐罐的5分钱买吃的。每到星期天晚上我都会走7里路，绕过大半个镇，只为去印度教的克利须那神庙吃顿好的，我爱极了那里的食物。就这样，我凭着自己的好奇与直觉，做着自己喜欢的事情。不过后来的事实证明，我当时所做的大部分事情，都成了我无比珍贵的经历。我举个例子来说吧：

当时里德学院的书法教育大概是全国最好的。校园内的每一张海报

---

stumble into　　无意中卷入；偶尔走入　　　　　　　calligraphy　n.　书法

classes, I decided to take a calligraphy class to learn how to do this. I learned about *serif* and san serif typefaces, about varying the amount of space between different letter combinations, about what makes great *typography* great. It was beautiful, historical, artistically subtle in a way that science can't capture, and I found it fascinating.

None of this had even a hope of any practical application in my life. But ten years later, when we were designing the first Macintosh computer, it all came back to me. And we designed it all into the Mac. It was the first computer with beautiful typography. If I had never dropped in on that single course in college, the "Mac" would have never had multiple typefaces or proportionally spaced *fonts*. And since Windows just copied the Mac, it's likely that no personal

---

上，每一个抽屉的标签上都是漂亮的手写体。因为我休学了，不用去上专业课，所以我便跑去上书法课。我学会了书写衬线字体与无衬线字体，学会了如何在不同字母组合间变更字间距，也了解到印刷术的伟大。书法的美感、历史感与艺术感是科学所无法捕捉的，我认为这是相当迷人的。

我从没有想过学这些东西会对我的生活起什么实际作用，不过10年后，当我在设计第一台苹果计算机时，我想起了当时所学到的东西，所以我把这些东西都融入了苹果的设计里，这便是第一台能打出漂亮字体的计算机。要不是我对书法课的热衷，苹果可能就不会有多重字体和等比例间

---

serif *n.* 衬线   typography *n.* （活版）印刷术
font *n.* 字体

computer would have them. If I had never dropped out, I would have never dropped in on that calligraphy class, and personal computers might not have the wonderful typography that they do. Of course it was impossible to connect the dots looking forward when I was in college. But it was very, very clear looking backwards 10 years later.

Again, you can't connect the dots looking forward; you can only connect them looking backwards. So you have to trust that the dots will somehow connect in your future. You have to trust in something—your *gut*, destiny, life, *karma*, whatever—because believing that the dots will connect down the road will give you the confidence to follow your heart, even when it leads you off the *well-worn* path, and that will make all the difference.

距字体了。要不是Windows 抄袭了苹果，要不是当年我休学去上书法课，大概所有的笔记本电脑里都不会出现我们所看到的这些漂亮字体。当然，我上大学时，不可能把这些点点滴滴预先串联在一起，但在10年后的今天，当我再回顾时，这一切都显得非常清楚。

再强调一次，你不可能事先将生命的点滴串联起来，充分预见其结果。只有当你回顾时，你才会发现这些点滴事物之间的联系。所以，要坚信，你现在所经历的，将会与你未来的生活串联起来。你不得不相信某些东西，你的直觉、命运、生活、因缘机会……正是由于这种信仰，我才没有失去希望，我的人生才会与众不同。

---

gut *n.* 胆量
well-worn *adj.* 用旧了的；陈腐的；平凡的

karma *n.* 缘分；命运

02

Three Stories from My Life II

Steve Jobs Stanford University Commencement Address, 2005

My second story is about love and loss.

I was lucky—I found what I loved to do early in life. Woz and I started Apple in my parents' *garage* when I was 20. We worked hard, and in 10 years Apple had grown from just the two of us in a garage into a two billion dollar

我人生中的三个故事 II

史蒂夫·乔布斯2005年在斯坦福大学毕业典礼上的演讲

我的第二个故事，是关于爱与失去。

我很幸运，因为我很早就知道自己的兴趣所在。20岁时，我和沃兹在我父母的车库里开创了苹果电脑公司。我们拼命工作，公司才得以在10年之间从一家在车库里只有两个小伙子的小作坊扩展成了一家员工超过4千人、资产达20亿美金的上市公司。在我30岁那年，我们提前一年推出

garage *n.* 车库

company with over 4,000 employees. We'd just released our finest creation—the Macintosh—a year earlier, and I had just turned 30.

And then I got fired. How can you get fired from a company you started? Well, as Apple grew we hired someone who I thought was very talented to run the company with me, and for the first year or so things went well. But then our visions of the future began to *diverge* and eventually we had a falling out. When we did, our *Board of Directors* sided with him. And so at 30, I was out. And very publicly out. What had been the focus of my entire adult life was gone, and it was *devastating*.

I really didn't know what to do for a few months. I felt that I had let the previous generation of *entrepreneurs* down—that I had

---

了公司最棒的产品——苹果计算机。

之后我就被解雇了。一个人怎么会被自己创办的公司解雇了呢？呃，随着苹果公司地不断壮大，我聘请了一个我认为很有才干的家伙来和我一起经营公司，他在开始的几年也确实干得不错。可是我们对未来的憧憬不同，所以最后只好分道扬镳，而董事会站在他那边，就这样在我30岁的时候，他们大张旗鼓地把我解雇了。多年来的心血和生活重心一下子都荡然无存了，我碰到了有生以来最残酷的打击。

有几个月，我真不知道要做些什么。我觉得我令业界的前辈们失望

---

diverge *v.* 分歧
devastating *adj.* 毁灭性的；令人震惊的

Board of Directors 董事会
entrepreneur *n.* 企业家

dropped the *baton* as it was being passed to me. I met with David Packard and Bob Noyce and tried to apologize for screwing up so badly. I was a very public failure, and I even thought about running away from the valley. But something slowly began to *dawn on* me: I still loved what I did. The turn of events at Apple had not changed that one bit. I had been rejected, but I was still in love. And so I decided to start over.

I didn't see it then, but it turned out that getting fired from Apple was the best thing that could have ever happened to me. The heaviness of being successful was replaced by the lightness of being a beginner again, less sure about everything. It freed me to enter one of the most creative periods of my life.

了，我把他们交给我的接力棒弄丢了。我试图向创办惠普公司的戴维·帕卡德和创办英特尔公司的鲍勃·诺宜斯道歉，告诉他们我很抱歉把事情搞砸了。我成了公众眼中失败的典范，甚至想要离开硅谷。但是渐渐地，我发现，我依旧喜欢我做过的那些事情。在苹果经历的那些事情丝毫没有让我改变自己的兴趣。虽然我被否定了，但我的兴趣没变，所以我决定从头再来。

当时我没发现，但现在看来，被苹果开除是我最好的经历。成功的压力被重新开始的轻松所取代，对每件事情都不那么确定，这件事让我轻松地走入我一生中最有创意的时期。

---

baton *n.* 接力棒　　　　　　　　dawn on　被理解；被领悟

During the next five years, I started a company named NeXT, another company named Pixar, and fell in love with an amazing woman who would become my wife. Pixar went on to create the world's first computer-animated feature film, *Toy Story*, and is now the most successful animation *studio* in the world. In a remarkable turn of events, Apple bought NeXT, and I returned to Apple, and the technology we developed at NeXT is at the heart of Apple's current *renaissance*. And Laurene and I have a wonderful family together.

I'm pretty sure none of this would have happened if I hadn't been fired from Apple. It was awful tasting medicine, but I guess the patient needed it. Sometime life—Sometimes life going to hit you in the head with a brick. Don't lose faith. I'm convinced that the only thing that kept me going was that I loved what I did. You've got to

---

接下来的5年里，我创立了 NeXT 公司，继而又创建了 Pixar 公司，同时也跟后来成为我妻子的劳伦恋爱了，她是个相当优秀的女人。Pixar 制作了世界上第一部全电脑动画电影《玩具总动员》，现在已经成为世界上最成功的动画制作公司。在一个非凡的转折时期，苹果收购了 NeXT，而我也回到了苹果。我们在 NeXT 研发的技术成了苹果后来复兴的核心部分。劳伦和我也组建了一个美满的家庭。

我很确定，如果当年没有被苹果开除，我就不会有今天的事业。良药苦口，有时候，生活会拿起砖头打你的头，但不要丧失信心。我确信我爱我的事业，这就是这些年来支持我继续走下去的唯一理由。所以你需要找

---

studio *n.* 工作室；制片厂；摄影棚   renaissance *n.* 复兴

find what you love.

And that is as true for your work as it is for your lovers. Your work is going to fill a large part of your life, and the only way to be truly satisfied is to do what you believe is great work. And the only way to do great work is to love what you do. If you haven't found it yet, keep looking—and don't settle. As with all matters of the heart, you'll know when you find it. And like any great *relationship*, it just gets better and better as the years roll on. So keep looking—don't settle.

出你的最爱。

选择人生伴侣是如此，工作也是如此。工作将占据你人生的一大部分，只有成就一番伟业你才会真正获得满足，而热爱你的工作是你成就伟业的唯一途径。如果你还没有找到自己热爱的事业，那就继续寻找，不要放弃。竭尽全力，你一定会找到。和其他事业一样，一切只会随着时间变得愈来愈好。所以，在你找到你所热爱的事业之前，请继续寻找，不要放弃。

relationship *n.* 关系；联系

03

Three Stories from My Life III

Steve Jobs Stanford University Commencement Address, 2005

My third story is about death. When I was 17, I read a *quote* that went something like: "If you live each day as if it was your last, someday you'll most certainly be right." It made an impression on me, and since then, for the past 33 years, I've looked in the mirror every morning and asked myself:

我人生中的三个故事 III

史蒂夫·乔布斯 2005 年在斯坦福大学毕业典礼上的演讲

我的第三个故事，是关于死亡。我17岁时，读到一则格言，好像是这样的："把每一天都当成生命中的最后一天来过，总有一天你会发现自己获益良多。"这句话对我影响很大，在过去的 33 年里，我每天早上都会对着镜子问自己："如果今天是我生命中的最后一天，我今天要做的事

---

quote *n.* 引语；语录

"If today were the last day of my life, would I want to do what I am about to do today?" And whenever the answer has been "No." for too many days in a row, I know I need to change something.

Remembering that I'll be dead soon is the most important tool I've ever encountered to help me make the big choices in life. Because almost everything—all external expectations, all pride, all fear of embarrassment or failure—these things just *fall away* in the face of death, leaving only what is truly important. Remembering that you are going to die is the best way I know to avoid the *trap* of thinking you have something to lose. You are already naked. There is no reason not to follow your heart.

About a year ago I was *diagnosed* with cancer. I had a scan at 7:30 in the morning, and it clearly showed a tumor on my *pancreas*. I didn't even know what a pancreas was. The doctors told me

情是我想做的吗？"一旦连续很多天我的答案都是一样的："不是。"我就知道我必须有所改变了。

当自己行将消亡一直都是我人生重大抉择时最重要的权衡砝码。因为几乎每件事，包括所有外界的期望、名声以及对困窘或失败的恐惧，在面对死亡时，全都不见了，只留下真正最重要的东西。告诉自己生命即将走到尽头是我所知道的避免掉入惧怕、失去漩涡的最好方法。当死亡来临时，你已经一无所有，没理由不去顺心而为。

一年前，我被诊断出患有癌症。我早上七点半作的扫描，胰腺部位清楚地出现了一个肿瘤，那时我甚至连胰腺是什么都不知道。医生告诉我，

fall away 消失；逐渐减少
diagnose v. 诊断；判断

trap n. 陷阱；困境
pancreas n. 胰腺

this was almost certainly a type of cancer that is incurable, and that I should expect to live no longer than three to six months. My doctor advised me to go home and get my affairs in order, which is doctor's code for "prepare to die". It means to try and tell your kids everything you thought you'd have the next 10 years to tell them in just a few months. It means to make sure everything is *buttoned up* so that it will be as easy as possible for your family. It means to say your goodbyes.

I lived with that diagnosis all day. Later that evening I had a *biopsy*, where they stuck an *endoscope* down my throat, through my stomach into my *intestines*, put a needle into my pancreas and got a

这基本上可以确认为不治之症，而且预计我最多可以活三到六个月。医生建议我回家，把身边的事处理好，这是医生对临终病人的标准建议。这就意味着你要在几个月内把你准备用十年的时间跟孩子讲的话都讲完，也意味着你要把每件事情都安排好，让家人尽量轻松地面对这一切，还意味着你要跟所有人说再见了。

我一整天都在想着那个诊断结果。晚上医生给我做了一次切片检查，从喉咙伸入一个内视镜，穿过胃进到肠道，将探针伸进胰腺，取了一些肿

button up　扣紧；顺利完成
endoscope　*n.* 内窥镜；内腔镜

biopsy　*n.* 切片检查
intestine　*n.* 肠

few cells from the *tumor*. I was *sedated*, but my wife, who was there, told me that when they viewed the cells under a microscope the doctors started crying because it turned out to be a very rare form of pancreatic cancer that is curable with *surgery*. I had the surgery and, thankfully, I'm fine now.

This was the closest I've been to facing death, and I hope it's the closest I get for a few more decades. Having lived through it, I can now say this to you with a bit more certainty than when death was a useful but purely intellectual concept: No one wants to die.

Even people who want to go to heaven don't want to die to get there. And yet death is the destination we all share. No one has ever escaped it. And that is as it should be, because Death is very likely

---

瘤细胞出来。我打了镇静剂，不省人事，但是我妻子在场。她后来对我说，当医生们通过显微镜检查那些细胞后，他们都哭了，因为那是一种非常罕见的胰脏癌，可以通过手术治愈。所以我接受了手术，谢天谢地现在已经康复了。

　　这是我面对死亡最近的一次，同时我也希望这是我在未来几十年里面对死亡最近的一次。经过此事后，死亡对我而言不仅仅只是纯粹的想象，而我也能更加肯定地告诉你们：没有人想死。

　　即使那些想上天堂的人，也想活着上天堂。但是死亡是我们共同的目的地，没有人能逃得过，这是注定的。也许在我们的生命中，死亡是最伟

---

tumor *n.* 肿瘤；肿块
surgery *n.* 外科；外科手术

sedate *v.* 给……施用镇静剂

MCGRAW-HILL

the single best invention of Life. It's Life's change agent. It clears out the old to make way for the new. Right now the new is you, but someday not too long from now, you will gradually become the old and be *cleared away*. Sorry to be so dramatic, but it's quite true.

Your time is limited, so don't waste it living someone else's life. Don't be trapped by dogma—which is living with the results of other people's thinking. Don't let the noise of others' opinions drown out your own inner voice. And most important, have the courage to follow your heart and intuition. They somehow already know what you truly want to become. Everything else is secondary.

大的创造，是生命交替的媒介，送走老人，给新生代让出道路。现在你们是新生代，但是不久的将来，你们也会变老，被送出人生的舞台。抱歉讲得这么夸张，但这是事实。

你们的时间是有限的，所以不要浪费时间为别人而活。不要被教条所限，活在别人的观念里。不要让别人的意见左右自己内心的声音。最重要的是，要勇敢地去追随自己的心灵和直觉，只有自己的心灵和直觉才知道你自己的真实想法，其他一切都是次要的。

---

clear away 把……清除掉

Hard Work and Determination Pays Off (Excerpt)

Arnold Schwarzenegger's Speech at Tsinghua University, 2005

After two or three years of *discipline* and determination and working out hard, I actually changed my body, and I changed my strength. And that told me something, that if I could change my body that much, then I could also change anything else. I could change

努力工作，决战人生（节选）

阿诺德·施瓦辛格 2005 年在清华大学的演讲

经过两三年意志上的磨炼和体力上的锻炼，我重塑了体格，力气也变大了。这件事告诉我，如果我能很大程度上改变体格，我就能改变一切：改变习惯、改变智力、改变态度、改变思想、改变未来、甚至改变人生。

discipline *n.* 训练；纪律

my habits, my intelligence, my attitude, my mind, my future, my life. And this is exactly what I've done. I think that lesson applies to people, and it also applies to countries. You can change, China can change, everyone in the world can change.

I remember the first time I went to the United States and I was competing in the World Championships in *Bodybuilding*. I lost and I was *devastated*. I felt like a loser, a major loser. I cried, as a matter of fact, because I felt like I disappointed my friends and I disappointed myself. But the next day I got my act together, I shifted *gears*, and I said, "I'm going to learn from that lesson." And from then on, I continued. My career took off, and everything that I wanted to do I accomplished. First it was to become a champion in bodybuilding. Later on I became a movie star, then I became the governor of the great state of California, of the sixth largest economy in the world.

事实上我已经做到了这一切。我想这一经验既适用于个人，也适用于国家。你能改变，中国能改变，世界上每一个人都能改变。

我还记得第一次到美国参加世界健美锦标赛时的情景。当时我输了，无比绝望。我就像一个失败者，一个彻底的失败者。我哭了，因为我感到我既让朋友失望了，也让自己失望了。但第二天，我重整旗鼓，转变态度，并对自己说，"我要吸取教训。"从那时起，我开始不断地努力，事业也从此飞黄腾达，我取得了自己想要的一切——首先我获得了健美冠军，随后我又成了一名电影明星，后来我还被任命为世界第六大经济体——加利福尼亚州的州长。

---

bodybuilding *n.* 健身
gear *n.* 齿轮；设备

devastated *adj.* 身心交瘁的；极为震惊的

All of this happened because of my dreams, even though other people told me that those dreams were *bogus* and they were crazy, but I held onto my dreams. In Hollywood, they said, "You will never make it. You have a German *accent*. No one in Hollywood has ever made it with a German accent. Yeah, maybe you can play some Nazi roles or something like that, but you cannot become a leading star with an accent. Plus your body, you're overdeveloped, you have all these muscles. They did Hercules movies 20 years ago, that's outdated. And your name, Schwarzenegger, it will never fit on a movie *poster*. Forget it, you will never make it. Go back to body building."

Well, the rest is history. After *Terminator 3*, I became the highest

---

实现这一切是因为我坚持了我的梦想，即使别人说我的那些梦想很疯狂而且不切实际，但我依然坚持不懈。在好莱坞的时候，他们曾说，"你不可能成功。因为你的英语带有德国口音，在好莱坞还没有一个大明星说话带德国口音的。饰演一些纳粹角色你倒是可以，但有口音的人想成为主角是不可能的。另外，你一身的肌肉，太过发达了！20年前他们的确拍过大力士的影片，不过早就过时了。还有你的名字，施瓦辛格，根本不适合上电影海报。算了，你不会成功的。还是回去继续你的健美运动吧！"

所有质疑都是过眼烟云。演完《终结者 III》之后，我便成了好莱坞

---

bogus *adj.* 假装的；假的   accent *n.* 口音；腔调
poster *n.* 招贴（画）；海报

paid movie star in Hollywood. And, let me tell you something, it continued on. Even when I ran for governor people said, "Arnold, you will never become governor of California. What do you know about government?" Well, I continued *campaigning*. I listened to my dreams, and the rest also is history. I became governor. So always it just carried me on, those dreams. So bodybuilding gave me the confidence, movies gave me the money, and public service and being a governor gave me a purpose larger than myself.

片酬最高的明星。但说实话，外界对我的质疑从未中断过。我竞选州长时还有人说，"阿诺，你永远不可能成为加州州长。你对政治了解多少？"但是我依旧参加了竞选。我相信自己的梦想，那些质疑声也都已成明日黄花，我最终当上了州长。梦想总是指引着我不断向前——健美运动给了我信心，电影给了我财富，而服务大众以及成为州长给了我更大的目标。

campaign *v.* 从事运动；作战

Unleashing Your Creativity

—Bill Gates

I've always been an *optimist* and I supposed that is rooted in my belief that the power of creativity and intelligence can make the world a better place.

For as long as I can remember, I've loved learning new things and solving problems. So when I sat down at a

---

释放你的创造力
——比尔·盖茨

我天性乐观，坚信人类凭借创造力和聪明才智可以让世界变得更加美妙，这一想法一直扎根于我的内心深处。

自从记事起，我便热衷于接触新事物，喜欢解决难题。可想而知，当我上7年级第一次坐在计算机前时，我是何等的着迷。那是一台锵锵作响的电传打字机，比我们今天拥有的计算机逊色很多，几乎一无所用，但正

---

optimist *n.* 乐观主义者

computer for the first time in seventh grade, I was *hooked*. It's was a *clunky* old *teletype* machine that barely do anything compared to the computer we have today. But it changed my life.

When my friend Paul Allen and I started Microsoft 30 years ago, we had a vision of "a computer on every desk and in every home", which probably sounded a little too optimistic at a time when most computers were the size of refrigerators. But we believe that personal computer would change the world. And they have.

And after 30 years, I'm still as inspired by computers as I was back in seventh grade.

I believe that computers are the most incredible tool we can use to feed our curiosity and inventiveness to help us solve problems that even the smartest people couldn't solve on their own.

是它改变了我的生活。

30年前，我和朋友保罗·艾伦创办微软时，我们的梦想是实现"让每个家庭、每张办公桌上都有一台计算机"，在计算机体积如同冰箱大小的年代，这个想法听起来似乎有点异想天开。但是我们相信个人电脑将改变世界。今天看来的确如此。

30年后，我仍然像上7年级那时一样对计算机狂热着迷。

我相信计算机是最神奇的工具，来满足我们的好奇心和发明创造的，甚至是最聪明的人凭自身力量无法应对的难题在计算机的帮助下都将迎刃而解。计算机已经改变了我们的学习方式，为世界各地的孩子们开启了一

---

hook *v.* 钩住　　　　　　　　　　　　　　　　　　clunky *adj.* 笨重的
teletype *n.* 电传打字机；电报交换机

UNLEASHING YOUR CREATIVITY

Computer have transformed how we learn, giving kids everywhere a window into all of the world's knowledge. They're helping us build communicates around the things we care about and to stay close to the people who are important to us, no matter where they are.

Like my friend Warren Buffett, I feel particularly lucky to do something every day I love to do. He calls it "tap-dancing to work". My job at Microsoft is as challenging as ever, but what makes me "tap-dancing to the work" is when we show people something new, like a computer that can recognize your handwriting or your speech, or one that can store a lifetime's worth of photos, and he say: "I didn't know you can do that with a PC!"

But for all the cool things that a person can do with a PC, there are lots of other ways we can put our *creativity* and intelligence to

扇通向大千世界知识的窗户。它可以为我们关注的事物建立"群"，让我们和那些对自己重要的人保持密切联系，不管他们身在何方。

就像我的朋友沃伦·布菲，每天都能做自己热爱的事情，我为此而感到无比幸运。他被称之为"跳着踢踏舞工作"的人。我在微软的工作永远充满挑战，但促使我一直坚持"跳着踢踏舞工作"的是我们向人们展示某些新成果的时刻，当他们看到计算机能识别笔迹、语音或者能存储值得保留一生的照片时就会赞不绝口："我不敢相信个人电脑竟可以如此万能。"

但是，除了可以用电脑做出很酷的事情之外，我们还可以通过许多别

creativity *n.* 创造力

MCGRAW-HILL
23

work to improve our world. There are still far too many people in the world whose most basic needs go *unmet*. Every year, for example, millions of people die from diseases that are easy to prevent or treat in the developed world.

I believe that my own good fortune brings with it a responsibility to give back to the world. My wife, Melinda, and I have committed to improving health and education in a way that can help as many people as possible.

As a father, I believe that the death of a child in Africa is no less *poignant* or tragic than the death of a child anywhere else. And that doesn't take much to make an immense difference in these children's lives.

I'm still very optimist, and I believe that progress on even the

---

的方式在工作中发挥自己的创造力和聪明才智，以此改善我们的世界。全球仍有许许多多的人还未解决最基本的生存需求。例如，每年仍有无数人死于那些在发达国家很容易预防而且能治疗的疾病。

我想，我所拥有的财富使我负有回馈社会的责任。我的妻子梅琳达和我尽可能多地致力于帮助人们改善健康和教育。

作为一个父亲，我认为，在非洲孩子的死给父亲带来的痛苦和悲伤丝毫不亚于其他任何地区。我认为，使这些孩子们的命运发生翻天覆地的变化并不会费太大力气。

我仍是一个坚定的乐观主义者，我坚信使世界级难题取得进展并解决

---

unmet *adj.* 未满足的   poignant *adj.* 令人痛苦的；辛酸的

world's toughest problems is possible and it's happening every day. We're seeing new drugs for deadly diseases, new *diagnostic* tools, and new attention paid to the health problems in the developing world.

I'm excited by the possibilities I see for medicine, for education and, of course, for technology. And I believe that through our natural inventiveness, creativity and willingness to solve tough problems, we're going to make some amazing achievements in all these areas in my lifetime.

都是有可能的——其实每天都在发生这种事情。我们看到治疗致命疾病的新药和新诊断器械在不断出现，发展中国家的健康问题也引起了人们的重视。

我为医药、教育，当然还有技术的诸多发展而感到欢欣鼓舞。我相信，人类凭借其与生俱来的发明创造能力和不畏艰难、坚忍不拔的品格，可以让我在有生之年看到我们在所有这些领域内创造出的可喜成就。

---

diagnostic *adj.* 诊断的；特征的

First Inaugural Address (Excerpt)

—John F·Kennedy

…

We observe today not a victory of party, but a celebration of freedom, symbolizing an end, as well as a beginning; signifying *renewal*, as well as change. For I have sworn before you and Almighty God the same *solemn* oath our *forebears prescribed* nearly a century and three quarters ago.

就职演讲（节选）

——约翰·F·肯尼迪

……

今天我们不是在庆祝一个政党的胜利，而是在庆祝自由的胜利。这象征着一个旧时代的结束和新时代的开始；意味着延续，也意味着变革。因为我已在你们和万能的上帝面前，宣读了我们的先辈在170多年前拟定的庄严誓言。

---

renewal *n.* 更新；恢复；革新；复苏
forebear *n.* 祖先；祖宗

solemn *adj.* 严肃的；庄严的
prescribe *v.* 指定；规定

In your hands, my fellow citizens, more than in mine, will rest the final success or failure of our course. Since this country was founded, each generation of Americans has been *summoned* to give *testimony* to its national loyalty. The graves of young Americans who answered the call to service surround the globe.

Now the trumpet summons us again, not as a call to bear arms, though arms we need; not as a call to battle, though embattled we are; but a call to bear the burden of a long twilight struggle, year in and year out, "rejoicing in hope; patient in *tribulation*", a struggle against the common enemies of man: *tyranny*, poverty, disease, and war itself.

公民们，掌握方针成败的不是我，而是你们。自从合众国建立以来，每一代美国人都曾受到召唤，保家卫国。那些响应号召为国而战献出自己生命的年轻人，他们的坟墓遍及全球。

现在，号角已经再次吹响——不是召唤我们拿起武器，尽管我们需要武器；不是召唤我们去作战，虽然我们严阵以待。而是召唤我们要担起重任，为黎明的到来作长期抗战。年复一年，"从希望中得到欢乐，在磨难中保持耐性"，为对付人类共同的敌人——专制、贫穷、疾病和战争而奋斗。

---

summon *v.* 召唤；传唤

tribulation *n.* 困难；灾难

testimony *n.* 证词；见证

tyranny *n.* 暴政；专制

Can we *forge* against these enemies a grand and global *alliance*, North and South, East and West, that can assure a more fruitful life for all mankind? Will you join in that historic effort?

In the long history of the world, only a few generations have been *granted* the role of defending freedom in its hour of maximum danger. I do not *shrink* from this responsibility. I welcome it. I do not believe that any of us would exchange places with any other people or any other generation. The energy, the faith, the devotion which we bring to this endeavor will light our country and all who serve it. And the glow from that fire can truly light the world.

And so, my fellow Americans, ask not what your country can do for you, ask what you can do for your country. My fellow citizens of

---

为抗击敌人，让人类丰衣足食，我们能够组成一个包括东西南北各方的全球大联盟吗？你们愿意加入这一历史性的事业吗？

在漫长的世界历史长河中，只有少数几代人遭遇了国难，担起了捍卫自由的责任。我不会推卸这一责任，相反，我很欢迎。我相信我们每一个人都会担起这个时代赋予的责任。我们为此所努力奉献的精力、信念和忠诚，将照亮我们的国家和所有为国效劳的人，而这火焰所发出的光芒也一定能照亮全世界。

因此，美国同胞们，不要问国家能为你们做些什么，而要问你们能为国家做些什么。全世界的同胞们，不要问美国能为你们做些什么，而要问

---

forge *v.* 锻造；锤炼
grant *v.* 授予；准予；同意

alliance *n.* 结盟；联盟
shrink *v.* 起皱；收缩；畏缩

the world, ask not what America will do for you, but what together we can do for the freedom of man.

Finally, whether you are citizens of America or citizens of the world, ask of us here the same high standards of strength and *sacrifice* which we ask of you. With a good conscience our only sure reward, with history the final judge of our deeds, let us go forth to lead the land we love, asking His blessing and His help, but knowing that here on earth, God's work must truly be our own.

我们能共同为人类的自由做些什么。

最后，不论你们是美国公民还是其他国家的公民，你们有权利要求我们竭尽全力乃至付出生命，当然，我们也是这样要求你们的。问心无愧是对我们的至高奖赏，历史是我们行动的最终裁判，让我们带领我们所热爱的国家，前进吧！让我们共同祈求上帝的福佑和帮助，因为我们知道，我们未来的事业就是上帝的旨意。

---

sacrifice *n.* 牺牲

07

Remarks in Shanghai Meeting with Future Chinese Leaders (Excerpt)

—Barack Hussein Obama

...

In addition to your growing economy, we admire China's extraordinary *commitment* to science and research—a commitment borne out in everything from the *infrastructure* you build to the technology you use. China is now the world's largest Internet user—which is why we were

上海会见青年学生的演讲（节选）

——巴拉克·侯赛因·奥巴马

......

　　我们不但钦佩中国日益增长的经济，也万分赞赏你们在科学研究方面做出的贡献——从你们建设的基础设施到你们所使用的技术，都是对此极好的诠释。中国目前是全球最大的互联网使用国——这也是我们把互联网作为此次活动一部分的原因。中国目前拥有全球最大的移动电话网络，而

---

commitment n. 承担的义务；保证；献身　　　infrastructure n. 结构；基础设施

so pleased to include the Internet as a part of today's event. This country now has the world's largest mobile phone network, and it is investing in the new forms of energy that can both sustain growth and *combat* climate change—and I'm looking forward to deepening the partnership between the United States and China in this critical area tomorrow. But above all, I see China's future in you—young people whose talent and dedication and dreams will do so much to help shape the 21st century.

I've said many times that I believe that our world is now fundamentally interconnected. The jobs we do, the *prosperity* we build, the environment we protect, the security that we seek—all of these things are shared. And given that interconnection, power in the 21st century is no longer a *zero-sum* game; one country's suc-

---

且目前正在投资发展新型能源，这既能维持可持续发展，又可以降低对气候的影响——我期待着在这个至关重要的领域内，美中两国的合作关系能在今后得到深化。总而言之，在你们身上，我看到了中国的未来——你们是年轻的一代，你们的聪明才智、献身精神和梦想将在建设21世纪的进程中发挥巨大作用。

我已多次谈到，而且我相信我们现在的世界是紧密相连的。我们所做的工作，我们所创建的盛世繁荣，所保护的环境，以及所追求的安全——所有这一切都是共有的。鉴于这种相互联系，在21世纪，权力不应再成为一场零和游戏，而且一国的成功发展不应以他国为代价。这就是美国为什

---

combat *v.* 与……斗争；与……战斗　　　　prosperity *n.* 兴旺；繁荣
zero-sum *adj.* 零和的

cess need not come at the expense of another. And that is why the United States insists we do not seek to contain China's rise. On the contrary, we welcome China as a strong and prosperous and successful member of the community of nations—a China that draws on the rights, strengths, and creativity of individual Chinese like you.

To return to the proverb—consider the past. We know that more is to be gained when great powers cooperate than when they *collide*. That is a lesson that human beings have learned time and again, and that is the example of the history between our nations. And I believe strongly that cooperation must go beyond our government. It must be rooted in our people—in the studies we share, the business that we do, the knowledge that we gain, and even in the sports that we

---

么坚决表示不会遏制中国崛起的原因。恰恰相反，我们欢迎中国成为国际社会中一个强大、繁荣、成功的成员——一个由所有中国人的努力、实力和创造力所创建的中国。

回到前面提到的那句成语——前车之鉴，后事之师。我们都知道，大国之间选择合作而非对抗会带来更大的利益。这是人类不断汲取的一个教训，在我们两国的关系史中也不乏其例。我深信，合作不能仅仅是政府间的合作。合作必须根植于我们的人民——根植于我们共同进行的研究、我们的商贸往来、我们所学的知识，乃至我们的体育运动。这些桥梁必须由

---

collide *v.* 碰撞；冲撞

play. And these bridges must be built by young men and women just like you and your *counterparts* in America.

That's why I'm pleased to announce that the United States will dramatically expand the number of our students who study in China to 100,000. And these exchanges mark a clear commitment to build ties among our people, as surely as you will help determine the destiny of the 21st century. And I'm absolutely confident that America has no better *ambassadors* to offer than our young people. For they, just like you, are filled with talent and energy and optimism about the history that is yet to be written.

我们两国的年轻人共同搭建，比如在座的各位。

因此，我非常高兴地宣布，美国将把到中国留学的学生人数大幅度增加到10万人，这种交流将为我们两国人民之间架设起友谊之桥梁。毫无疑问，21世纪的未来将由你们决定。我完全相信，对美国来说，最好的使者莫过于我们的年轻一代。因为他们和你们一样，才华横溢、活力四射，对即将书写的历史篇章充满乐观。

---

counterpart *n.* 与对方地位作用相当的人（或物）

ambassador *n.* 大使；使节

08

The Fringe Benefits of Failure, and the Importance of Imagination I

J. K. Rowling's Address in Harvard University, 2008

Looking back at the 21-year-old that I was at graduation, is a slightly uncomfortable experience for the 42-year-old that she has become. Half my lifetime ago, I was *striking* an uneasy balance between the ambition I had for myself, and what those closest to me

失败的好处和想象力的重要性 I
J. K. 罗琳 2008 年在哈佛大学的演讲

回顾21岁时刚踏出校门的自己，对于42岁的我来说，那段经历并不愉快。换句话说，在我人生的前半部分，我都挣扎于自己的满腔抱负和身边人对我的期望之间。

---

strike *v.* 达到（两全其美）；找到（折中办法）

expected of me.

I was convinced that the only thing I wanted to do, ever, was to write novels. However, my parents, both of whom came from *impoverished* backgrounds and neither of whom had been to college, took the view that my overactive imagination was an amusing personal quirk that could never pay a *mortgage*, or secure a pension. They had hoped that I would take a *vocational* degree; I wanted to study English Literature. A *compromise* was reached that in retrospect satisfied nobody, and I went up to study Modern Languages. Hardly had my parents' car rounded the corner at the end of the road than I ditched German and scuttled off down the Classics corridor.

I cannot remember telling my parents that I was studying Classics; they might well have found out for the first time on

---

我知道自己唯一想做的事情就是写小说。不过，我的父母自幼生活贫困，而且没有念过大学，所以在他们看来，我过度的想象力，可让人开怀一笑，但根本不足以让我支付按揭，让他们老有所依。他们希望我能读专业学位，而我想攻读英国文学。最后，尽管我们彼此妥协，但双方都不是很满意：我改学了现代语言。可是等我父母一走开，我就立刻放弃了德语而报名学习古典文学。

我记得当时我并没将这事告诉父母，他们可能是在参加我的毕业典礼时才得知此事的。我想，他们肯定会认为，在万千专业中，不会有比研究

---

impoverished *adj.* 贫困的   mortgage *n.* 抵押；抵押借款
vocational *adj.* 职业的   compromise *n.* 妥协；折中

graduation day. Of all the subjects on this planet, I think they would have been hard put to name one less useful than Greek mythology when it came to securing the keys to an executive bathroom.

I would like to make it clear, in *parenthesis*, that I do not blame my parents for their point of view. There is an *expiry* date on blaming your parents for steering you in the wrong direction; the moment you are old enough to take the wheel, responsibility lies with you. What is more, I cannot criticise my parents for hoping that I would never experience poverty. They had been poor themselves, and I have since been poor, and I quite agree with them that it is not an *ennobling* experience. Poverty entails fear, and stress, and sometimes depression; it means a thousand petty *humiliations* and hardships. Climbing out of poverty by your own efforts, that is indeed something on which to pride yourself, but poverty itself is romanticised only by fools.

希腊神话更没用的专业了，连一间独立宽敞的卫生间都换不来。

不过，我想澄清一下：我不会因为父母的观点而责怪他们。埋怨父母给你指错方向是有一个时间段的。一旦当你长大，可以掌握自己人生方向的时候，你就得承担起责任。我更不会因父母不希望我生活拮据，而责怪他们。他们的生活一直很贫困，我也曾一度很穷，所以我很理解他们。贫穷并不能使人变得高尚，相反，会让人感到恐惧、压力、有时还会绝望，贫穷意味着无尽的羞辱和艰辛。靠自己的努力摆脱贫穷，的确是件引以为傲的事，只有傻瓜才会对贫穷本身夸夸其谈。

---

parenthesis *n.* 插入语；括弧

ennoble *v.* 使尊贵；使杰出

expiry *n.* 满期；逾期

humiliation *n.* 羞辱；屈辱

What I feared most for myself at your age was not poverty, but failure.

At your age, in spite of a distinct lack of motivation at university, where I had spent far too long in the coffee bar writing stories, and far too little time at lectures, I had a *knack* for passing examinations, and that, for years, had been the measure of success in my life and that of my peers.

I am not dull enough to suppose that because you are young, gifted and well-educated, you have never known hardship or heartache. Talent and intelligence never yet inoculated anyone against the caprice of the Fates, and I do not for a moment suppose that everyone here has enjoyed an existence of unruffled *privilege*

我在你们这个年龄时最害怕的不是贫穷，而是失败。

像你们这么大时，我也在念大学，但是缺乏学习动力。我大多时候都在咖啡馆写故事，几乎不怎么去上课。但是我有一个诀窍，知道如何顺利通过考试，正因如此我在大学期间的成绩并不比别人差。

我不会蠢到说，因为你们年轻、有天分，而且受过良好的教育，所以没有遭遇过挫折和心碎。其实拥有才华和智慧，并不能让你对命运的变数未雨绸缪。我想在座的各位都不仅仅满足于当前。相反，哈佛毕业生的身

---

knack *n.* 特殊能力；窍门   privilege   *n.* 特权

and contentment. However, the fact that you are graduating from Harvard suggests that you are not very well-acquainted with failure. You might be driven by a fear of failure quite as much as a desire for success. Indeed, your conception of failure might not be too far from the average person's idea of success, so high have you already flown *academically*.

份，意味着你们对失败不会有切身体会。也许你们渴求成功，但同时也惧怕失败。说实话，你们眼中的失败，在普通人眼中可能已经是成功，毕竟你们在学业上已经达到很高的高度了。

academically *adv.* 学术上；理论上

The Fringe Benefits of Failure, and the Importance of Imagination II

J·K·Rowling's Address in Harvard University, 2008

Ultimately, we all have to decide for ourselves what constitutes failure, but the world is quite eager to give you a set of criteria if you let it. So I think it fair to say that by any conventional measure, a mere seven years after my graduation day, I had failed on an *epic*

失败的好处和想象力的重要性 II
J. K. 罗琳 2008 年在哈佛大学的演讲

最终，我们需要给失败下个定义，但只要你愿意，这个世界非常渴望给你一套标准。公平地讲，从任何传统标准来看，在毕业后仅仅七年的时间里，我的失败可谓空前绝后：短暂的婚姻闪电般破裂，而且我还失业

epic *n.* 史诗；叙事诗

scale. An exceptionally short-lived marriage had *imploded*, and I was jobless, a lone parent, and as poor as it is possible to be in modern Britain, without being homeless. The fears my parents had had for me, and that I had had for myself, had both come to pass, and by every usual standard, I was the biggest failure I knew.

Now, I am not going to stand here and tell you that failure is fun. That period of my life was a dark one, and I had no idea that there was going to be what the press has since represented as a kind of fairy tale resolution. I had no idea how far the tunnel extended, and for a long time, any light at the end of it was a hope rather than a reality.

So why do I talk about the benefits of failure? Simply because failure meant a stripping away of the inessential. I stopped

了，这一切使我成了一名举步维艰的单身母亲。除了不至于无家可归之外，我可以算得上是当代英国最穷的人，几乎一无所有。当年父母和我自己对未来的担忧，现在都变成了现实。按照一般标准来看，我是我所知道的最失败的人。

现在，站在这里，我不会告诉你们失败很有趣。那是我生命中一段黑暗的日子，我不知道它是否是童话故事里必须要历经的磨难，也不知道自己还要在黑暗中走多久。有很长一段时间，照亮前方的任何光芒都只是希望而不是现实。

那么，为什么我还要讨论失败的好处呢？简单来说是因为失败可以剥

implode *v.* 内爆；剧减

pretending to myself that I was anything other than what I was, and began to direct all my energy into finishing the only work that mattered to me. Had I really succeeded at anything else, I might never have found the determination to succeed in the one area I believed I truly belonged. I was set free, because my greatest fear had been realised, and I was still alive, and I still had a daughter whom I *adored*, and I had an old typewriter and a big idea. And so rock bottom became the solid foundation on which I rebuilt my life.

You might never fail on the scale I did, but some failure in life is *inevitable*. It is impossible to live without failing at something, unless you live so cautiously that you might as well not have lived at all, in which case, you fail by default.

掉那些不是很重要的东西。我不再伪装自己，而是开始正视自我，把所有精力放在对我最重要的事情上。如果不是在其他领域的失败，我不会下定决心，在一个我确信真正属于我的舞台上取得成功。我摆脱了束缚，因为在经历了人生中最大的梦魇后，我还活着，而且还有一个深爱的女儿、一台旧打字机和一个很大的梦想。所以困境的谷底成为我重建生活的坚实基础。

你们可能永远不会经历像我那样的失败，但有些失败，是生活中不可避免的。生活不可能一帆风顺，除非你活得万般小心，而那样的话，你便和没来过这个世界没什么两样。

---

adore *v.* 崇拜；爱慕；非常喜欢   inevitable *adj.* 不可避免的；必然（发生）的

Failure gave me an inner security that I had never attained by passing examinations. Failure taught me things about myself that I could have learned no other way. I discovered that I had a strong will, and more discipline than I had suspected; I also found out that I had friends whose value was truly above the price of rubies.

The knowledge that you have emerged wiser and stronger from *setbacks* means that you are, ever after, secure in your ability to survive. You will never truly know yourself, or the strength of your relationships, until both have been tested by *adversity*. Such knowledge is a true gift, for all that it is painfully won, and it has been worth more to me than any qualification I ever earned.

So given a Time Turner, I would tell my 21-year-old self that

---

失败给了我内心的安宁，而这种安宁是顺利通过考试的人无法获得的。失败让我认清了自己，这些是没法从其他地方学到的。而且我发现，我比自己想象中更坚强，更有决心。此外我还发现，我拥有比珠宝更加珍贵的朋友。

从挫折中获得的知识越充满智慧、越有力，你在以后的生存中就会越安全。只有历经磨难，你们才会真正认识自己，真正了解身边的人。这些知识才是真正的礼物，比我曾获得的任何资格证书都更为珍贵，因为这是我饱尝艰辛痛苦后获得的。如果给我一部时间机器，我会告诉21岁的自己，人的幸福在于明白生活不是一份漂亮的成绩单，你的资历和简历也不

---

setback n. 挫折；倒退　　　　　　　　　　　　adversity n. 不幸

personal happiness lies in knowing that life is not a check-list of acquisition or achievement. Your qualifications, your CV, are not your life, though you will meet many people of my age and older who confuse the two. Life is difficult, and complicated, and beyond anyone's total control, and the humility to know that will enable you to survive its *vicissitudes*.

是你的生活，当然你会碰到很多与我同龄或更老一点的人今天依然还在混淆两者。生活是艰辛的、复杂的，不是个人能完全掌控的，所以谦恭地认识到这一点后，你的生活会更好。

vicissitude　*n.*　（人生的）盛衰；变迁

10

The Fringe Benefits of Failure, and the Importance of Imagination Ⅲ

J. K. Rowling's Address in Harvard University, 2008

And yet I also learned more about human goodness at *Amnesty International* than I had ever known before.

Amnesty *mobilises* thousands of people who have never been *tortured* or imprisoned for their beliefs to act *on behalf of* those who have. The power

---

失败的好处和想象力的重要性 Ⅲ

J. K. 罗琳 2008 年在哈佛大学的演讲

同时，在国际特赦组织中我也看到了人类的善良，比我想象中的要多很多。

大赦国际动员成千上万因为个人信仰而没有受到折磨或监禁的人，去

Amnesty International   国际特赦组织   mobilise *v.* 动员；赋予可动性

torture *v.* 拷问；折磨   on behalf of   代表；为了

of human *empathy*, leading to *collective action*, saves lives, and frees prisoners. Ordinary people, whose personal well-being and security are assured, join together in huge numbers to save people they do not know, and will never meet. My small participation in that process was one of the most *humbling* and inspiring experiences of my life.

Unlike any other creature on this planet, human beings can learn and understand, without having experienced. They can think themselves into other people's places.

Of course, this is a power, like my brand of fictional magic, that is morally neutral. One might use such an ability to *manipulate*, or control, just as much as to understand or sympathise.

为那些遭受不幸的人奔走。人类心灵相通的力量，激发集体行动，拯救生命，解放囚犯。个人的福祉和安全有保证的普通百姓需要携手合作，拯救那些素不相识，甚至也许永远都不会见面的人。我用自己微薄的力量参与了这次活动，而这成为我一生中最令人振奋的体验。

与这个星球上任何其他生物不同的是，人类可以学习和理解未曾经历过的东西。他们可以将心比心、设身处地地理解他人。当然，这种能力，就像在我虚构的魔法世界里一样，在道德上是中立的。

一个人可能会利用这种能力去操纵或者控制他人，而有些人却选择去了解或同情他人。

---

empathy *n.* 心意相通；（感情等）融为一体　　collective action　集体行动
humbling *adj.* 令人羞辱的　　manipulate *v.* 操纵；控制

And many prefer not to exercise their imaginations at all. They choose to remain comfortably within the bounds of their own experience, never troubling to wonder how it would feel to have been born other than they are. They can refuse to hear screams or to *peer* inside cages; they can close their minds and hearts to any suffering that does not touch them personally; they can refuse to know.

I might *be tempted to* envy people who can live that way, except that I do not think they have any fewer nightmares than I do. Choosing to live in narrow spaces can lead to a form of mental *agoraphobia*, and that brings its own terrors. I think the wilfully unimaginative see more monsters. They are often more afraid.

很多人选择不去使用他们的想象力，他们宁愿留在自己舒适的世界里，也不愿花力气去想想如果出生在别处会怎样。他们不愿意去听别人的尖叫，或去看一眼囚笼。只要痛苦不触及他们自己，他们就会可以封闭自己的内心，从而选择明哲保身。

我有时会羡慕那样生活的人，但我想他们做的噩梦并不会比我少。生活在狭窄的空间，会令人不敢面对开阔的视野，因为那会给自己带来恐惧。我认为不愿展开想象的人会看到更多的怪兽，这会使他们感到更害

---

peer *v.* 仔细看   be tempted to 被诱惑去做；总想做
agoraphobia *n.* 广场恐惧症；旷野恐惧症

What is more, those who choose not to empathise may enable real monsters. For without ever committing an act of *outright* evil ourselves, we collude with it, through our own apathy.

One of the many things I learned at the end of that Classics *corridor* down which I ventured at the age of 18, in search of something I could not then define, was this, written by the Greek author Plutarch: What we achieve inwardly will change outer reality.

That is an astonishing statement and yet proven a thousand times every day of our lives. It expresses, in part, our inescapable connection with the outside world, the fact that we touch other people's lives simply by existing.

But how much more are you, Harvard graduates of 2008, likely

怕。那些不愿给予同情的人，甚至可能会激活真正的怪兽。因为尽管他们自己并没有犯下罪恶，但我们却通过冷漠与之勾结。

我从18岁开始徜徉于古典文学的海洋中，学到的其中一件事就是希腊作家普鲁塔克曾说过的这样一句：我们对内在修养的追求将会改变外在现实。当时的我并不能完全理解这番话。

那其实是一个惊人的论断，曾被我们的生活无数次证实。它指出我们与外部世界有无法脱离的联系，我们通过触摸着他人的生命而存在。

但是，哈佛大学的2008届毕业生们，你们中有多少人可能去触及他

outright *adj.* 完全的；彻底的　　　　　　corridor *n.* 走廊；通道

to touch other people's lives? Your intelligence, your capacity for hard work, the education you have earned and received, give you unique status, and unique *responsibilities*. Even your nationality sets you apart. The great majority of you belong to the world's only remaining superpower. The way you vote, the way you live, the way you protest, the pressure you bring to bear on your government, has an impact way beyond your borders. That is your privilege, and your burden.

If you choose to use your status and influence to raise your voice on behalf of those who have no voice; if you choose to identify not only with the powerful, but with the powerless; if you retain the ability to imagine yourself into the lives of those who do not have your advantages, then it will not only be your proud families who

---

人的生命？你们的智慧，你们努力工作的能力，以及你们所受到的教育，都给予了你们独特的地位和责任。甚至连你们的国籍也让你们与众不同，你们中的绝大部分人属于这个世界上唯一的超级大国。你们的表决方式、生活方式、抗议方式及给政府带来的压力，都具有超乎寻常的影响力。这是你们的特权，也是你们的责任。

如果你们选择利用自己的地位和影响，去为那些没有发言权的人发言；如果你们选择不仅与强者为伍，还会同情帮扶弱者；如果你们会设身

---

responsibitity *n.* 责任

celebrate your existence, but thousands and millions of people whose reality you have helped to change. We do not need magic to *transform* the world, we carry all the power we need inside ourselves already: we have the power to imagine better.

处地为不如你们的人着想，那么你的存在，将不仅是你们家人的骄傲，更是无数因为你们的帮助而改变命运的人的骄傲。我们不需要用魔法来改变世界，因为我们的内心已经拥有了足够的力量：我们有能力做得更好！

transform *v.* 改变

Message of Hope(Excerpt)

Nick Vujicic's Address on the 2010 FIFA World Cup South Africa

I was born different. But that doesn't stop me from living my life. And I'm happy.

I love soccer so much and I don't play as well as others, of course. But you know, in the World Cup, there is so much *anticipation* and excitement that *stirs up* in all of us and everybody

播撒希望（节选）

尼克·胡哲致2010年南非世界杯演讲

我一出生就和别人不一样，但这并不影响我过属于自己的生活，而且我的生活很幸福。

我非常喜欢足球，当然，我踢得没有别人好。不过在世界杯期间，我们所有人都会对比赛充满期待和渴望，每个人都为自己球队的胜利而欢

anticipation n. 预期；预料　　　　　　　　　　　stir up 激起；挑起

cheers for this success of their own team. And you know in all games there is losing and winning. People who moan over, you know, their team not winning and then people who get so excited when they win. Everybody loves to win but we shall not linger on the difference between winning and losing. At the World Cup, most of the fans around the world will experience the loss of their team. But is losing failing?

At age 8, I wanted to end my life. I told my mom I wanted to commit suicide. And then, age 10, I actually tried. I felt like I had no hope to live. I felt like I was so different to everybody else, and there was definitely no future or hope for me.

If I gave up, thinking that that was the end, I would have *missed out* on so much more. Life is life. There are lots of successes but also lots of failures and it repeats itself again and again. Should we really

---

呼。但是只要是比赛就会有胜负，你们肯定知道失败一方的球迷会感到悲伤，而胜利一方的球迷则激动万分。每个人都渴望胜利，但我们不应该过多地关注输赢。在世界杯期间，大多数球迷都将经历本方球队的失利，可是输球就意味着失败吗？

8岁时，我想结束生命，所以我告诉母亲我想自杀。而10岁那年，我确实尝试过自杀。那时，我根本没有活下去的希望。我感觉自己和别人不一样。对我而言，生活没有未来，也没有希望。

如果当时我放弃了，认为生命该就此终结的话，那我就会错失许多东西。生活就是生活，有得也有失，周而复始。难道每次经历所谓的失败我

---

miss out 错过机会

despair every time we go through, you know a failure?

You're saying "oh, now I am a failure for the rest of my life." You see, the stairs right in front of me are a huge *barrier* and one step at a time is what I have to do. If I never try, I'll never achieve anything. If I fall down, what do I do? I am gonna try again and again because the moment I give up is the moment that I'll fail. It is so important that we don't despair with the results that we sometimes don't anticipate whether it's in the soccer game or life. So *embrace* the path your team has taken and believe that they will try again with *resilience*. Then you will feel the happiness in life again to be able to enjoy the World Cup as a true festival as it is, a celebration. Failure is not important. How you overcome it is.

们就要心生绝望吗？

你会说：“噢，如今我的余生都将在失败中度过。”你看，我面前的阶梯就是巨大的障碍，我必须一步一步走上去。如果我不尝试，就会永远一事无成。如果我摔倒了，我该怎么做？我会一次又一次地尝试，因为放弃就意味着失败。不要为结果而绝望，这很重要，因为无论是在足球比赛场上还是在生活中，我们都无法预料下一秒将会发生什么。因此，坦然接受自己球队的比赛结果吧，相信他们还会继续顽强拼搏的。那样你就能够再次感受到生活的快乐，能够把世界杯当作真正的节日去庆祝。失败并不重要，如何战胜失败才是最重要的。

---

barrier *n.* 障碍物　　　　embrace *v.* 拥抱
resilience *n.* 弹性；弹力

12

Beautiful Smile and Love (Excerpt)

Nobel Peace Prize Acceptance Speech by Mother Teresa, Oslo, Norway, 1979

The poor are very wonderful people. One evening we went out and we picked up four people from the street. And one of them was in a most terrible *condition*, and I told the sisters: You take care of the other three. I take care of this one who looked worse. So I did for her all that my love can do. I put her

美丽的微笑和爱（节选）

特蕾莎修女1979年在诺贝尔和平奖颁奖大会上的演讲

贫穷的人是非常了不起的人。一天晚上我们外出的时候，从街上带回了四个人，其中一个人的生命岌岌可危。于是我告诉修女们说："你们照料其他三个，我来照顾这个濒危的人。"就这样，我为她做了我所能做

condition   *n.* 状况；状态

in bed, and there was such a beautiful smile on her face. She took hold of my hand as she said just the words "thank you" and she died. I could not help but examine my conscience before her and I asked what would I say if I was in her place. And my answer was very simple. I would have tried to draw a little attention to myself. I would have said I am hungry, that I am dying, I am cold, I am in pain, or something, but she gave me much more—she gave me her grateful love. And she died with a smile on her face. As did that man whom we picked up from the *drain*, half eaten with worms, and we brought him to the home. "I have lived like an animal in the street, but I am going to die like an angel, loved and cared for." And it was so wonderful to see the greatness of that man who could speak

---

的一切。我将她放在床上时，看到她的脸上绽露出非常美丽的微笑。她握着我的手，只说了句"谢谢您"就离开了人世。我不禁在她面前审视起自己的良知。我问自己，如果我是她，我会说些什么呢？答案很简单，我会尽量引起别人对我的关注，我会说我饥饿难忍、冷得发抖、奄奄一息、痛苦不堪，诸如此类的话。但是她给我远不止这些，她给了我她真挚的感激之情。临走时脸上还带着微笑。我们从水渠边带回的那个男子也是如此。当时，他的全身几乎都快被虫子吃掉了，我们把他带回了家。"在街上，我像动物一样活着，但我却可以像个天使一样死去，因为有人爱，有人关心。"我看到了他的伟大之处，他可以说出那样的话，真是太奇妙了。他

---

drain *n.* 排水沟

like that, who could die like that without blaming anybody, without cursing anybody, without comparing anything. Like an angel—this is the greatness of our people. And that is why we believe what Jesus had said: I was hungry, I was naked, I was homeless, I was unwanted, unloved, uncared for, and you did it to me.

I believe that we are not real social workers. We may be doing social work in the eyes of the people, but we are really *contemplatives* in the heart of the world. For we are touching the body of Christ twenty-four hours... And I think that in our family we don't need bombs and guns, to destroy, to bring peace, just get together, love one another, bring that peace, that joy, that strength of presence of each other in the home. And we will be able to overcome all the evil

离开人世时，不责怪任何人，也不诅咒任何人，无欲无求，就像天使一样——这便是我们人民的伟大之处。因此我们相信耶稣所说的话：我饥肠辘辘，我衣不蔽体，我无家可归，我不为人所要，不为人所爱，也不为人所关心，然而，你却为我做了这一切。

其实，我们算不上真正的社会工作者。或许在别人的眼中我们是在做社会工作，但实际上，我们真的只是世界中心的修行者。因为，一天 24 小时，我们都在触摸基督的圣体。我想，在我们的大家庭里，我们不需要枪支和炮弹来破坏和平，或带来和平，我们只需要团结起来，彼此相爱，将和平、欢乐以及每一个家庭成员的灵魂的力量凝结，就能战胜世界上现

contemplative *n.* 修行者；沉思冥想的人

that is in the world.

And with this prize that I have received as a Prize of Peace, I am going to try to make the home for many people who have no home. Because I believe that love begins at home, and if we can create a home for the poor I think that more and more love will spread. And we will be able through this understanding love to bring peace be the good news to the poor. The poor in our own family first, in our country and in the world. To be able to do this, our Sisters, our lives have to be wove with *prayer*. They have to be woven with Christ to be able to understand, to be able to share. Because to be woven with Christ is to be able to understand, to be able to share. Because today there is so much suffering... When I pick up a person from the street, hungry, I give him a plate of rice, a piece of bread, I have

---

存的一切邪恶。

我准备用我所获得的诺贝尔和平奖奖金为那些无家可归的人们建立自己的家园，因为我相信，爱源自家庭。如果我们能为穷人建立家园，我想爱会传播得更广。而且，传播这种宽容博大的爱，会给世界带来和平，成为穷人的福音。首先是为我们自己家里的穷人，其次为我们国家，而后是为全世界的穷人。姐妹们，为了做到这一点，我们的生活就必须与祷告紧紧相连，必须同基督结为一体才能互相体谅、共同分享，因为同基督结合一体就意味着互相体谅、共同分享。因为，今天的世界上仍有如此多的苦难存在……当我从街上带回一个饥肠辘辘的人时，给他一碗饭，一片面

---

prayer *n.* 祈祷，祷告

satisfied. I have removed that hunger. But a person who is *shut out*, who feels unwanted, unloved, terrified, the person who has been thrown out from society—that poverty is so full of hurt and so unbearable... And so let us always meet each other with a smile, for the smile is the beginning of love, and once we begin to love each other naturally we want to do something.

包，他就心满意足了，因为我能驱除他的饥饿。但是，如果一个人露宿街头，感到不为人所要，不为人所爱，惶恐不安，被社会抛弃，这样的贫穷让人心痛，更令人无法忍受。因此，让我们微笑面对彼此，因为微笑是爱的开端，一旦我们开始相亲相爱，我们就会想着为对方做点什么了。

---

shut out　把……排斥在外

13

Concession Speech I (Excerpt)

—— Hillary Diane Rodham Clinton

...

You have inspired and touched me with the stories of the joys and sorrows that make up the *fabric* of our lives and you have *humbled* me with your commitment to our country.

18 million of you from *all walks of life*—women and men, young and old, *Latino* and Asian, African-American and

退选演讲 I（节选）

——希拉里·黛安·罗德姆·克林顿

......

你们生活中有悲有喜的故事鼓励着我、感动着我。与你们为国家所做的贡献相比，我显得无比卑微。

1800万来自各行各业的男男女女，老老少少，拉丁血统或亚裔朋友、黑人朋友和高加索人民、富人、穷人、中产阶级、同性恋者或异性恋

---

fabric *n.* 织物；织品
all walks of life 各行各业；各界人士

humble *v.* 使谦恭
Latino *n.* 拉丁美洲人

Caucasian, rich, poor and middle class, gay and straight—you have stood strong with me. And I will continue to stand strong with you, every time, every place, and every way that I can. The dreams we share are worth fighting for.

Remember—we fought for the single mom with a young daughter, *juggling* work and school, who told me, "I'm doing it all to better myself for her." We fought for the woman who grabbed my hand, and asked me, "What are you going to do to make sure I have health care?" and began to cry because even though she works three jobs, she can't afford insurance. We fought for the young man in *the Marine Corps* T-shirt who waited months for medical care and said, "Take care of my *buddies* over there and then, will you please

---

者，你们曾与我一起并肩作战。无论何时何地，我都会尽我所能，一如既往地和你们站在一起，因为让你我为之奋斗的是我们共同的梦想！

请记住，我们曾经为了那个带着小孩拼命工作学习的单身母亲而奋斗过。她曾对我说："我做的一切都是为了让我女儿过得更好。"我们曾为了那个握住我的手的女士奋斗过。她曾问道："你怎样做才能确保我能享受医疗保障？"她边说边哭，因为即使她同时做三份工作也无力承担医药费。我们曾为了那位身穿海军T恤苦等了数月在医院治疗的小伙子奋斗过。他说："照顾照顾我那边的朋友吧！同时也能不能顺便照顾一下我？"我们曾为了所有失去工作、无法支付医药费、加不起油、买不起日

Caucasian n. 高加索人；白种人
the Marine Corps 海军陆战队

juggle v. 尽力应付
buddy n. 伙伴；兄弟；好朋友

help take care of me?" We fought for all those who've lost jobs and health care, who can't afford gas or groceries or college, who have felt invisible to their president these last seven years.

I entered this race because I have an old-fashioned conviction: that public service is about helping people solve their problems and live their dreams. I've had every opportunity and blessing in my own life—and I want the same for all Americans. Until that day comes, you will always find me on the front lines of democracy—fighting for the future.

The way to continue our fight now—to accomplish the goals for which we stand—is to take our energy, our passion, our strength and do all we can to help elect Barack Obama the next President of the United States.

Today, as I *suspend* my *campaign*, I congratulate him on the victory

---

常用品、上不起大学却在过去的7年里被总统忽视的人们奋斗过。

　　我参加此次选举是因为我始终怀着一个传统的信念，那就是公共服务是用来解决人们的困难以及实现人们的梦想的。我抓住了生命中的一切机会和上天的福佑，同时希望所有的美国人都能如此。在那一天到来之前，你永远会看见我始终都站在民主的最前线，为了未来而奋斗！

　　现在，为了能够继续我们的奋斗、实现我们坚持的目标的方法，我们要竭尽全能、满怀激情且全力以赴地支持巴拉克·奥巴马，我们的下一任美国总统。

　　今天，在我退出竞选的时刻，我想对奥巴马所取得的胜利以及他奋斗

---

suspend *v.* 暂停；中止　　　　　　　　campaign *n.* （社会，政治）运动；活动

he has won and the extraordinary race he has run. I *endorse* him, and throw my full support behind him. And I ask all of you to join me in working as hard for Barack Obama as you have for me.

I have served in the Senate with him for four years. I have been in this campaign with him for 16 months. I have stood on the stage and gone *toe-to-toe* with him in 22 debates. I have had a front row seat to his *candidacy*, and I have seen his strength and determination, his grace and his *grit*.

In his own life, Barack Obama has lived the American Dream. As a community organizer, in the state senate, as a United States Senator—he has dedicated himself to ensuring the dream is realized. And in this campaign, he has inspired so many to become involved in the democratic process and invested in our common future.

至今所赢得的不凡成绩表示祝贺，我将在他身后全力支持他。我要你们所有人一起，像支持我一样地支持奥巴马。

我在参议院和他一起工作了 4 年，一起参加了 16 个月的选举，而且站在台上和他面对面进行了 22 场辩论。我曾坐在他候选演讲的最前排，看到过他的力量和决断、他的风度和刚毅。

巴拉克·奥巴马在他自己的生命中，作为政体的组织者实现着美国人的梦想；在参议院，作为国家参议员，他把实现国人梦想作为自己的毕生追求；在竞选中，他鼓舞着无数人为推进民主进程和创建我们共同的未来而努力着。

---

endorse *v.* 赞同；支持

candidacy *n.* 候选人的地位；候选资格

toe-to-toe *adj.* 用近战方式的；近距离的

grit *n.* 勇气；坚毅

13

Concession Speech II (Excerpt)

——Hillary Diane Rodham Clinton

Now, on a personal note when I was asked what it means to be a woman *running for* President, I always gave the same answer: that I was proud to be running as a woman but I was running because I thought I'd be the best President. But I am a woman, and like millions of women, I know there are still

退选演讲 II（节选）

——希拉里·黛安·罗德姆·克林顿

每当有人问起，竞选总统对一个女人来说意味着什么时，我的回答总是相同的，那就是作为女人，我为参加总统竞选而感到自豪。我参加竞选是因为我认为我会成为最好的总统，但我是一个女人，和众多女人一样，面临许多障碍和偏见，虽然有些并非有意为之。所以我想建立一个能够尊

run for 竞选

barriers and *biases* out there, often unconscious. I want to build an America that respects and embraces the potential of every last one of us.

I ran as a daughter who benefited from opportunities my mother never dreamed of. I ran as a mother who worries about my daughter's future and a mother who wants to lead all children to brighter tomorrows. To build that future I see, we must make sure that women and men alike understand the struggles of their grandmothers and mothers, and that women enjoy equal opportunities, equal pay, and equal respect. Let us resolve and work toward achieving some very simple *propositions*: There are no acceptable limits and there are no acceptable *prejudices* in the twenty-first century. You can be so proud that, from now on, it

---

重和包容我们每个人潜力的伟大国家。

作为一个女儿，我得益于许多我母亲从未梦想过的机会。作为一个母亲，我担心我女儿的未来，同时我也想给所有孩子一个更加光明的未来。为了创建设想中的未来，我们要让所有的男女同胞都能理解他们祖母和母亲几代人的努力，那就是女性要与男性拥有平等的机会、平等的报酬和平等的尊重。让我们下定决心努力坚持实现一个简单的愿望：21世纪的美国，没有对妇女的限制，也没有偏见。你以此为傲，从现在起，女性从某

---

bias *n.* 偏见；偏心　　　　　　　proposition *n.* 主张；建议；提案
prejudice *n.* 偏见；成见

will be *unremarkable* for a woman to win primary state victories, unremarkable to have a woman in a close race to be our nominee, unremarkable to think that a woman can be the President of the United States. And that is truly remarkable.

To those who are disappointed that we couldn't go all the way especially the young people who put so much into this campaign it would break my heart if, in falling short of my goal, I in any way discouraged any of you from pursuing yours. Always aim high, work hard, and care deeply about what you believe in. When you *stumble*, keep faith. When you're knocked down, get right back up. And never listen to anyone who says you can't or shouldn't go on.

As we gather here today in this historic magnificent building, the 50th woman to leave this Earth is orbiting overhead. If we can *blast*

州脱颖而出不值一提，女性获选举提名不值一提，女性成为美利坚合众国总统也不值一提。可是，我的朋友，下面这些绝对值得一提。

对我们没能走完全程而失望，特别是倾注了大量心血的年轻人来说，我在目标未实现之际就出局了，倘若你们因我的出局而放弃追求才是真正令我心碎的。志存高远、兢兢业业、坚持理想的朋友们，遭遇障碍时，请不要放弃信念，在哪跌倒就在哪爬起来，不要听信任何人所谓的你不行、不要继续下去的说法。

我们今天聚集在这座历史悠久、富丽堂皇的建筑物里，而世界上第50位登上太空的女性正在我们上空按轨道运行。我们既然能将50位女性

unremarkable *adj.* 平凡的；不出色的　　　　stumble *v.* 绊倒；跌跌撞撞地走
blast *v.* 爆炸

50 women into space, we will someday *launch* a woman into the White House.

Although we weren't able to *shatter* that highest, hardest glass ceiling this time, thanks to you, it's got about 18 million cracks in it. And the light is shining through like never before, filling us all with the hope and the sure knowledge that the path will be a little easier next time.

送入太空，却为何不能将一位女性送入白宫？

　　尽管此时此刻我们还不能粉碎头顶上坚硬的天花板，但托你们的福，它上面已经有了1800万条裂缝。前所未有的光明从中渗入进来，照亮我们，带给我们希望和信心——坚信下一次道路会平坦很多。

---

launch *v.* 发动；推出　　　shatter *v.* 粉碎；砸碎；使破灭

Concession Speech III(Excerpt)
——Hillary Diane Rodham Clinton

That has always been the history of progress in America. Think of the *suffragists* who gathered at Seneca Falls in 1848 and those who kept fighting until women could cast their votes. Think of the who struggled and died to see the end of slavery. Think of the civil rights heroes and *foot-soldiers* who

退选演讲 Ⅲ（节选）
——希拉里·黛安·罗德姆·克林顿

美国曾经的进步都已成为历史。想想1848年，聚集在塞尼卡福尔斯为了女性能拥有选举权而不懈奋斗的选民们，想想为取消奴隶制而奋斗至生命的最后一刻的革命先辈们；想想为消除种族隔离而示威游行、抗议，

---

suffragist *n.* 妇女政权论者　　　　　　　　　　foot-soldier *n.* 步兵

marched, protested and risked their lives to bring about the end to *segregation* and *Jim Crow*.

Because of them, I grew up taking for granted that women could vote. Because of them, my daughter grew up taking for granted that children of all colors could go to school together. Because of them, Barack Obama and I could *wage* a hard fought campaign for the Democratic *nomination*. Because of them, and because of you, children today will grow up taking for granted that an African American or a woman can, yes, become President of the United States.

When that day arrives and a woman takes the oath of office as our President, we will all stand taller, proud of the values of our nation, proud that every little girl can dream and that her dreams can

---

将生命置之度外的人权运动的英雄和军人们。

正因为有他们，我才能成长在女性选举权获得承认的时代；正因为有他们，我女儿才能成长在不同肤色的孩子们可以一起上学的时代；正因为有他们，奥巴马和我才可以参加民主党提名这样一场激烈的竞选；正因为有他们和你们，孩子们才可以成长在黑人和女性都可以当总统的时代。

当一个女人宣誓成为总统的那一天来临时，我们将站得更高，将会为我们国家的价值观而自豪，为每个美国小姑娘都能拥有梦想并实现梦想而

---

segregation *n.* 隔离

wage *v.* 开展；进行（战争、运动）

Jim Crow 〈贬〉黑人

nomination *n.* 提名；指派

come true in America. And all of you will know that because of your passion and hard work you helped pave the way for that day.

So I want to say to my supporters, when you hear people saying or think to yourself "if only" or "what if", I say, "please don't go there." Every moment wasted looking back keeps us from moving forward.

Life is too short, time is too *precious*, and the stakes are too high to dwell on what might have been. We have to work together for what still can be. And that is why I will work my heart out to make sure that Senator Obama is our next President and I hope and pray that all of you will join me in that effort.

To my supporters and colleagues in Congress, to the governors

---

自豪。你们会明白，是你们用满满的激情和艰苦奋斗才编织出这美好蓝图的。

因此我想对我的支持者说：当你听到有人想说或你自己想说"如果……该多好"或"要是……就好了"时，我想说，请一定不要这样。每次回望过去都会阻碍我们向前迈进的步伐。

人生短暂，逝者如斯，专注于改变现有既定模式，赌注实在太高，我们应为未来而共同奋斗。这就是我为何要全力支持奥巴马成为下一任总统的原因。我希望并祈盼我们所有人都能为之而共同努力。

我的支持者和议会的同事们、政府官员和市长们以及参加竞选的官员们，感谢你们无论成败都与我站在一起，谢谢你们的支持和领导。

---

precious   *adj.* 贵重的；宝贵的

and mayors, elected officials who stood with me, in good times and in bad, thank you for your strength and leadership.

To my friends in our labor unions who stood strong every step of the way I thank you and *pledge* my support to you.

To my friends, from every stage of my life your love and *ongoing* commitments *sustain* me every single day.

To my family especially Bill and Chelsea and my mother, you mean the world to me and I thank you for all you have done.

And to my extraordinary staff, volunteers and supporters, thank you for working those long, hard hours. Thank you for dropping everything leaving work or school travelling to places you'd never been, sometimes for months on end. And thanks to your families as well because your sacrifice was theirs too. All of you were there for

---

劳工联盟中的朋友们，谢谢你们坚持与我一路同行，我也会全力支持你们的。

我人生舞台上的每一位朋友，感谢你们给予我的爱和始终如一的奉献支撑我度过了每一天。

亲爱的家人们，特别是比尔、切尔西还有我的妈妈，你们是我的全部，我对你们所做的一切表示深深地谢意。

我优秀的员工们、志愿者们、支持者们，谢谢你们为我努力了这么长时间，谢谢你们所放弃的一切，你们离乡背井，千里迢迢来到这个陌生的地方，有时一待便是数月。也谢谢你们的家人，你们所做出的牺牲也是他

---

pledge *v.* 保证；许诺　　　　　　　　ongoing *adj.* 继续的
sustain *v.* 供养；支持

me every step of the way.

Being human, we are imperfect. That's why we need each other. To catch each other when we *falter*. To encourage each other when we lose heart. Some may lead; others may follow; but none of us can go it alone.

The changes we're working for are changes that we can only accomplish together. Life, liberty, and the pursuit of happiness are rights that belong to each of us as individuals. But our lives, our freedom, our happiness, are best enjoyed, best protected, and best advanced when we do work together.

们的牺牲，你们所有人都与我一路走来。

作为人类，我们都不完美。所以我们需要互相帮助，步履蹒跚时需要互相扶持，失去信心时需要互相鼓励。前者呼，后者应，没有人可以踽踽独行。

只有共同努力我们才能取得变革。我们每个人都拥有追求生命、自由以及幸福的权利，只要齐心协力，我们就能最大限度地享受生命、享受自由、享受幸福，并最好的保护我们享有的这一切。

---

falter *n.* （嗓音）颤抖；犹豫；蹒跚

15

Nobel Prize Acceptance Speech

——William Faulkner

I feel that this award was not made to me as a man, but to my work—a life's work in the *agony* and sweat of the human spirit, not for glory and least of all for profit, but to create out of the materials of the human spirit something which did not exist before. So this award is only mine in trust. It will not be

---

诺贝尔文学奖获奖演说

——威廉·福克纳

　　我认为这个奖项不是授予我个人而是授予我的工作——人类精神的工作，这是我毕生从事的关于人类精神的呕心沥血的工作。我从事这项工作，不为名、不图利，只为从人类精神原料中创造一些前所未有的东西。因此这个奖项我只是代为保管。为奖金及其本身的目的和意义而致辞并非

---

agony　*n.*　（极度的）痛苦；创痛

difficult to find a *dedication* for the money part of it *commensurate* with the purpose and significance of its origin. But I would like to do the same with the *acclaim* too, by using this moment as a *pinnacle* from which I might be listened to by the young men and women already dedicated to the same anguish and travail, among whom is already that one who will some day stand here where I am standing.

Our tragedy today is a general and universal physical fear so long sustained by now that we can even bear it. There are no longer problems of the spirit. There is only the question: When will I be blown up? Because of this, the young man or woman writing today has forgotten the problems of the human heart in conflict with itself which alone can make good writing because only that is worth writing about, worth the agony and the sweat.

He must learn them again. He must teach himself that the

难事。但我还想利用这一时刻，利用这个举世瞩目的讲坛，向献身于同一艰苦事业的青年男女致敬，有一天他们中必定会有人站在我今天所站的这个位置。

　　现在我们的悲剧是人们普遍长期存在一种生理上的恐惧，而我们对此早已习惯了。如今已不存在精神上的问题，只存在一个问题——我何时会被炸得粉身碎骨？因此，如今年轻人的作品开始抛弃对人类内心冲突的描写，然而他们所抛弃的却是一篇好作品中的精华。因为只有这种冲突才值得写作，值得忍受煎熬，值得付出汗水。

　　人一定要了解这些，一定要让自己认识到世间最可鄙之事莫过于恐

---

dedication　*n.* 奉献；献词；献堂礼　　　　commensurate　*adj.* 同样大小的；相称的

acclaim　*n.* 称赞；欢迎　　　　　　　　pinnacle　*n.* 顶点

basest of all things is to be afraid; and, teaching himself that, forget it forever, leaving no room in his workshop for anything but the old *verities* and truths of the heart, the old universal truths lacking which any story is *ephemeral* and *doomed*—love and honor and pity and pride and *compassion* and sacrifice. Until he does so, he labors under a curse. He writes not of love but of lust, of defeats in which nobody loses anything of value, of victories without hope and, worst of all, without pity or compassion. His grieves grieve on no universal bones, leaving no scars. He writes not of the heart but of the glands.

Until he relearns these things, he will write as though he stood among and watched the end of man. I decline to accept the end of man. It is easy enough to say that man is immortal simply because he will endure: that when the last ding-dong of doom has clanged

---

惧，一定要告诫自己永远地忘却恐惧，一定要让除了心灵正直诚实以外任何东西有容身之处。如果缺乏爱、荣誉、怜悯、自尊、同情与牺牲等感情，任何小说都只能如昙花一现，不会成功。若非如此，一切都将会是徒劳的。这样的小说中，男女主人公之间流露出的是情欲而非爱情；失败中无人失去可贵之物，而胜利中又毫无希望、甚至毫无怜悯或同情；没有刻骨铭心的悲伤；描写的不是心灵深处而是分泌腺体的器官。

在人们重新了解这些之前，他们的写作，就犹如站在世界末日中去观察末日的来临。我不赞同人类会走向灭亡，因为人类因能忍耐而不朽。当命运的最后钟声敲响，当傍晚最后一抹红色从平静无浪的礁石退去时，万

---

verity *n.* 真实性

doom *v.* 注定；命定

ephemeral *adj.* 朝生暮死的；生命短暂的

compassion *n.* 同情；怜悯

and *faded* from the last worthless rock hanging tideless in the last red and dying evening, that even then there will still be one more sound: that of his *puny* inexhaustible voice, still talking. I refuse to accept this. I believe that man will not merely endure: he will prevail. He is immortal, not because he alone among creatures has an inexhaustible voice, but because he has a soul, a spirit capable of compassion and sacrifice and endurance.

The poet's, the writer's duty is to write about these things. It is his privilege to help man endure by lifting his heart, by reminding him of the courage and honor and hope and pride and compassion and pity and sacrifice which have been the glory of his past. The poet's voice need not merely be the record of man, it can be one of the *props*, the pillars to help him endure and prevail.

物静寂，但是人类微弱而不倦的声音却还在争鸣。我不赞同这种说法，因为我相信人类不仅能忍耐，而且还会取得胜利。人类是不朽的，不是因为世界万物中唯人拥有不倦的声音，而是因为人拥有灵魂，拥有能够同情、牺牲、忍耐的精神。

诗人和作家的职责就是书写这些精神。他们有幸通过鼓舞人的斗志，提醒人们牢记昔日的荣耀：勇气、荣誉、希望、尊严、同情、怜悯以及牺牲精神，以使人类不朽。诗人的声音不仅是对人类的简单记录，还应起到支柱作用，帮助人类去延续去发展。

---

fade *v.* 褪去

prop *n.* 支柱；支撑物；支撑

puny *adj.* 弱小的；发育不良的

16

Unite to Create Prosperous Tomorrow

——Gordon Brown

I was with Nelson Mandela a year ago when he was in London. I was at a concert that he was attending to mark his birthday and for the creation of new resources for his foundation. I was sitting next to Nelson Mandela—I was very *privileged* to do so—when Amy Winehouse came onto the stage

联合起来，共创美好未来
　　——戈登·希朗

　　一年前我在伦敦见到了纳尔逊·曼德拉，我们当时正出席一个音乐会，庆祝曼德拉生日和他的基金会获得新资源。我当时就坐在曼德拉的身边——我对此感到非常荣幸。当看到艾米·怀恩豪斯登上舞台的时候，曼

privileged *adj.* 有特权的；享受特殊待遇的

and Nelson Mandela was quite surprised at the appearance of the singer and I was explaining to him at the time who she was. Amy Winehouse said, "Nelson Mandela and I have a lot in common. My husband too has spent a long time in prison." Nelson Mandela then went down to the stage and he summarized the challenge for us all. He said in his lifetime he had climbed a great mountain, the mountain of challenging and then defeating *racial oppression* and defeating *apartheid*. He said that there was a greater challenge ahead, the challenge of poverty, of climate change, global challenges that needed global solutions and needed the creation of a truly global society.

We are the first generation that is in a position to do this. Combine the power of a global ethic with the power of our ability

---

德拉显得有点吃惊，我便向他解释艾米·怀恩豪斯是何许人物。艾米·怀恩豪斯在舞台上说道："我和曼德拉有很多共同之处。我丈夫也曾经很长一段时间被关在监狱里。"随后曼德拉走向舞台，概述了我们现在所面临的挑战。他说，在他有生之年里，他攀越了一座无比陡峭的高山，充满挑战并且最终击败了种族压迫与隔离。他认为前方还有更为艰巨的挑战等待着我们——贫穷和气候变化。这些全球性的挑战需要全球性的解决方案，需要创造一个真正全球化的社会。

而我们是有能力实现这一切的第一代。将一个全球性的道德理念与全球性的沟通能力和组织能力相结合，来共同面对那些全球性的挑战。一

---

racial *adj.* 人种的；种族的　　　　　　　oppression *n.* 压迫；镇压
apartheid *n.* 种族隔离

to communicate and organize globally with the challenges that we now face, most of which are global in their nature. Climate change cannot be solved in one country but has got to be solved by the world working together. A financial crisis, just as we have seen, could not be solved by America alone or Europe alone; it needed the world to work together. Take the problems of security and *terrorism* and, equally, the problem of human rights and development: they cannot be solved by Africa alone; they cannot be solved by America or Europe alone. We cannot solve these problems unless we work together.

So the great project of our generation, it seems to me, is to build for the first time out of a global ethic and our global ability to communicate and organize together, a truly global society, built on that ethic but with *institutions* that can serve that global society and

---

个国家无法解决气候变化问题，但是如果全世界同心协力、彼此合作，问题就会迎刃而解。正如我们所亲眼看见的一样，仅仅依靠美国或者欧洲是无法解决金融危机的，它需要全世界的共同努力。另外国家安全与恐怖主义问题，抑或是与其同等重要的人权与发展问题，依然无法单靠非洲就能独立解决，也不能单独依靠美国或是欧洲，而是需要全世界通力合作来解决。

所以，在我看来，我们这一代人最重要的工作就是有史以来第一次通过全球性的道德观以及沟通与组织能力，建立一个以道德规范为基础的全球化的社会，并与为其服务的各类机构一起开创一个不一样的未来。我们

---

terrorism *n.* 恐怖主义；恐怖行动   institution *n.* 社会公共机构；制度

make for a different future. We have now, and are the first generation with, the power to do this. Take climate change. Is it not absolutely *scandalous* that we have a situation where we know that there is a climate change problem, where we know also that that will mean we have to give more resources to the poorest countries to deal with that, when we want to create a global *carbon* market, but there is no global institution that people have been able to agree upon to deal with this problem? One of the things that has to come out of *Copenhagen* in the next few months is an agreement that there will be a global environmental institution that is able to deal with the problems of persuading the whole of the world to move along a climate-change agenda.

正是第一代有能力实现这一切的人。例如，我们正面临严峻的气候变化问题，而我们知道如果真想创建一个全球性的"碳市场"，就需要给贫穷国家捐赠更多的资源，帮助他们来处理这一问题。但话虽如此，我们仍然没有一个可以值得信赖认可的全球性机构来解决这个问题，这不是相当滑稽可笑的事情吗？几个月后气候会议将在哥本哈根举行，此次会议须达成的协议之一就是建立一个全球性环境机构，来敦促整个世界为了气候变化的进程而共同行动起来。

scandalous *adj.* 不道德的；可耻的   carbon *n.* 碳
Copenhagen *n.* 哥本哈根（丹麦首都）

17

First Inaugural Address (Excerpt)

——Franklin Delano Roosevelt

Happiness lies not in the mere possession of money. It lies in the joy of achievement, in the *thrill* of creative efforts, the joy and moral *stimulation* of work no longer must be forgotten in the mad chase of *evanescent* profits. These dark days, my friends, will be worth

第一次就职演说（节选）

——富兰克林·德拉诺·罗斯福

　　幸福不只是单纯拥有金钱，而在于获得成就时的喜悦以及产生创造力时的激情，在于为疯狂追逐转瞬即逝的利润而工作所带来的难以忘却的愉悦和激励。如果这些黯淡的日子能使我们认识到，我们真正的使命不是要别人侍奉，而是要为自己和同胞们服务的话，那么，我们所付出的代价就

---

thrill　*n.* 兴奋；引起激动的事物　　　　　　stimulation　*n.* 刺激；激励；鼓舞
evanescent　*adj.* 短暂的；瞬息的

all they cost us, if they teach us that our true destiny is not to be ministered on to, but to minister to ourselves, to our fellow men.

Recognition of the falsity of material wealth as the standard of success goes hand in hand with the abandonment of a false belief that public office and high political position are to be valued only by the standards of pride of place and personal profits, and there must be an end to our conduct in banking and in business, which too often has given to a sacred trust the likeness of *callous* and selfish wrong-doing. Small wonder that confidence *languishes*, for it thrives only on honesty, on honor, on the sacredness of our obligation, on faithful protection and on unselfish performance. Without them it cannot live.

Restoration calls, however, not for changes in *ethics* alone. This

---

是完全值得的。

一旦认识到不能以物质财富为衡量成功的标准后，我们就会摒弃以地位和个人收益为唯一标准来衡量公职和政治高位的错误信念。我们必须制止银行界和企业界利用神圣的委托而进行无情、自私的不正当行为。为何我们的信心在减弱？因为只有诚实、信誉、忠心维护和无私的作为才能鼓舞信心，如果没有这一切，信心也就不复存在。

但是，复兴需要改变，而且不仅仅是伦理观念的改变。国家需要行动起来，而且现在就要行动起来。

---

callous *adj.* 无情的　　　　　　　languish *v.* 衰弱无力；失去活力
restoration *n.* 修复　　　　　　　ethics *n.* 伦理学

nation is asking for action, and action now.

Our greatest primary task is to put people to work. This is no unsolvable problem if we take it wisely and courageously. It can be accomplished in part by direct *recruiting* by the government itself, treating the task as we would treat the emergency of a war, but at the same time, through this employment, accomplishing greatly needed projects to stimulate and reorganize the use of our great natural resources.

Hand in hand with that, we must frankly recognize the overbalance of population in our industrial centers and by engaging on a national scale in a redistribution in an effort to provide better use of the land for those best fitted for the land.

Yes, the task can be helped by definite efforts to raise the value

---

我们的当务之急就是让人们有工作可做。只要我们充分利用智慧和勇气，这个问题就可以解决。一方面，政府可以直接征募人手，就像对待临战的紧要关头一样，另外这些人员也可以完成急需的工程，从而促进和改组我们对自然资源的利用。

坦白地说，我们要认识到工业中心现在面临人口失衡，所以我们要齐心协力，必须在全国范围内重新分配，使土地在最适合的人手中发挥更大的作用。

为了促成此项工作，可通过采取具体措施提高农产品价格，从而提

---

recruit *v.* 招募；吸收

of the agricultural product and with this the power to purchase the output of our cities. It can be helped by preventing realistically, the tragedy of the growing losses through fore closures of our small homes and our farms. It can be helped by insistence that the federal, the state, and the local government act *forthwith* on the demands that their costs be *drastically* reduce. It can be helped by the unifying of relief activities which today are often scattered, uneconomical, unequal. It can be helped by national planning for, and supervision of all forms of transportation, and of communications, and other utilities that have a definitely public character. There are many ways in which it can be helped, but it can never be helped by merely talking about it. We must act, we must act quickly.

高对城市产品的购买力；可切实避免因取消小作坊、农场抵押品赎回权所造成的悲剧和日益严重的损失；可坚持通过联邦和各州以及各地方政府采取行动而支持大量削减抵押的要求。可把救济工作统一掌管起来以避免目前的分散、浪费和分布不均的现象；可把一切形式的交通运输和其他明确属于公用事业的设施置于国家计划和监督之下。总之，可以促成此项工作的方法有很多，唯有空谈无用。所以我们必须行动起来，而且立即行动起来！

---

forthwith *adv.* 立刻   drastically *adv.* 大幅度地；彻底地

18

Harvard Commencement **A**ddress **I**(Excerpt)

——Steven Chu

...

My address will follow the classical *sonata* form of commencement addresses. The first movement, just presented, were *light-hearted* remarks. This next movement consists of *unsolicited* advice, which is rarely valued, seldom remembered, never followed. As Oscar Wilde said, "The

---

哈佛毕业典礼演讲 Ⅰ（节选）
　　——朱棣文

......

　　毕业演讲一般都遵循古典奏鸣曲的乐章，我的演讲也不例外。刚才是第一乐章——轻快的闲谈。接下来的第二乐章是不请自来的忠告，鲜受重视，少被铭记，也从不被遵从。但是，就像奥斯卡·王尔德所讲的：

---

sonata *n.* 奏鸣曲　　　　　　　　　light-hearted *adj.* 轻松的；无忧无虑的
unsolicited *adj.* 未经邀请的；主动提供的

only thing to do with good advice is to pass it on. It is never of any use to oneself." So, here comes the advice. First, every time you celebrate an achievement, be thankful to those who made it possible. Thank your parents and friends who supported you, thank your professors who were *inspirational*, and especially thank the other professors whose less-than-brilliant lectures forced you to teach yourself. Going forward, the ability to teach yourself is the *hallmark* of a great *liberal arts* education and will be the key to your success. To your fellow students who have added immeasurably to your education during those late night discussions, hug them. Also, of course, thank Harvard. Should you forget, there's an *alumni* association to remind you. Second, in your future life, cultivate a

---

"对于忠告，你所要做的，就是传递给别人，因为忠告对个人而言，毫无用处。"所以，下面就是我的忠告。第一，取得成就的时候，不要忘记前人。要感谢你的父母和支持你的朋友，感谢那些启发过你的教授，尤其是那些上不好课的教授，因为是他们迫使你自学。从长远看，自学能力是优秀人文科学教育的标识，是你成功的关键。拥抱你的同学，并感谢他们多次陪你彻夜长谈，给你的教育带来了无法衡量的价值。当然，你还要感谢哈佛。不过即使你忘了这一点，校友会也会提醒你的。第二，在你们未来的人生中，做一个慷慨大方的人。在任何谈判中，都不要为了最后那一点

---

inspirational *adj.* 鼓舞人心的
liberal arts *n.* 人文科学

hallmark *n.* 品质证明；标志；特征
alumnus *n.* 校友（pl.alumni）

generous spirit. In all negotiations, don't bargain for the last, little advantage. Leave the change on the table. In your *collaborations*, always remember that "credit" is not a *conserved* quantity. In a successful collaboration, everybody gets 90 percent of the credit.

Jimmy Stewart, as Elwood P. Dowd in the movie *Harvey* got it exactly right. He said: "Years ago my mother used to say to me,'In this world, Elwood, you must be...' she always used to call me Elwood '... in this world, Elwood, you must be oh so smart or oh so pleasant.'" Well, for years I was smart... I recommend pleasant. You may quote me on that.

My third piece of advice is as follows: As you begin this new stage of your lives, follow your passion. If you don't have a passion,

---

点利益而斤斤计较，留一点好处给对方。在合作中，不要想着独占荣誉。在一次成功的合作中，任何一方都应获得全部荣誉的 90%。

电影《迷离世界》中，吉米·斯图尔特扮演的角色埃尔伍德·奥多德就完全明白了这点。他说："多年前，母亲曾对我说，'埃尔伍德，活在这个世上，你要么做一个聪明人，要么做一个好人。'"我做聪明人已经好多年了。……但是，我给你们的建议是，做个好人。你们可以重复我这句话。

我的第三个忠告是，当你步入人生新的阶段时，请追随你的热情。如果没有热情，就去寻找，不找到就不罢休。生命太短暂，不能得过且过，

---

collaboration *n.* 合作；协作　　　　　　conserve *v.* 保护；保藏

don't be satisfied until you find one. Life is too short to go through it without caring deeply about something. When I was your age, I was *incredibly* single-minded in my goal to be a physicist. After college, I spent eight years as a graduate student and postdoc at Berkeley, and then nine years at Bell Labs. During that my time, my central focus and professional joy was physics.

Here is my final piece of advice. Pursuing a personal passion is important, but it should not be your only goal. When you are old and gray, and look back on your life, you will want to be proud of what you have done. The source of that pride won't be the things you have acquired or the recognition you have received. It will be the lives you have touched and the difference you have made.

你必须对某样东西倾注你的全部热情。在你们这个年龄,我是一个超级一根筋,我的目标就是非成为物理学家不可。本科毕业后,我在加州大学伯克利分校又待了8年,读完了研究生和博士后,然后去贝尔实验室工作了9年。这些年中,我关注的焦点以及职业上的全部乐趣,都来自物理学。

我还有最后一个忠告,追求个人名利固然重要,但这不应该成为你唯一追求的目标。当你白发苍苍、垂垂老矣而回首人生时,你会想要为你的过往感到自豪。让你产生自豪感的不会是你所拥有的名和利,而是那些曾经受你影响且被你改变过的人和事。

---

incredibly *adv.* 不可思议的;难以置信的

19

Harvard Commencement **A**ddress **Ⅱ**(Excerpt)

——Steven Chu

The Obama administration is laying a new foundation for a prosperous and *sustainable* energy future, but we don't have all of the answers. That's where you come in. In this address, I am asking you,the Harvard graduates, to join us. As our future intellectual leaders, take the time to learn more

哈佛毕业典礼演讲 Ⅱ（节选）
——朱棣文

奥巴马政府正在为未来能源的繁荣和可持续发展开创新的基础。但是我们还有很多力不能及之处，这就需要你们来施展抱负。在这次演讲中，我请求在座各位哈佛毕业生们，加入我们，成为我们中的一员。你们是未来充满睿智的领袖，请花点时间加深对目前危险局势的理解，并采取相应的行动。

sustainable *adj.* 可持续的；合理利用的

about what's at stake, and then act on that knowledge. As future scientists and engineers, I ask you to give us better technology solutions. As future economists and political scientists, I ask you to create better policy options. As future business leaders, I ask that you make sustainability an *integral* part of your business.

Finally, as humanists, I ask that you speak to our common humanity. One of the cruelest ironies about climate change is that the ones who will be hurt the most are the most innocent: the world's poorest and those yet to be born.

The *coda* to this last movement is borrowed from two humanists.

The first quote is from Martin Luther King. He spoke on ending the war in *Vietnam* in 1967, but his message seems so fitting for today's climate crisis:

"This call for a worldwide fellowship that lifts neighborly concern

---

你们是未来的科学家和工程师，可以给我们提供更好的技术方案。你们是未来的经济学家和政治家，可为我们开创更好的政策格局。你们是未来的企业家，请务必将可持续发展作为你们工作中不可分割的一部分。

最后，你们是人道主义者，请一定要站在人道主义的立场上讲话。对气候变化最残酷的讽刺之一就是，受伤害的人恰恰就是最无辜的人——那些世界上最贫穷的人和那些尚未出生的人。

我将引用两位人道主义者的话作为这个乐章的完结。

第一段话引自马丁·路德·金。这是1967年他对结束越南战争的评论，但看上去非常适合用来评论今天的气候危机。

"我呼吁全世界的人们团结一心，抛弃种族、肤色、阶级、国籍的隔

---

integral *adj.* 构成整体所必需的；基本的   coda *n.* 乐章结尾部；完结部
Vietnam *n.* 越南

beyond one's *tribe*, race, class, and nation is in reality a call for an *all-embracing* and unconditional love for all mankind. This of tmisunderstood, this oft misinterpreted concept, so readily *dismissed* by the Nietzsches of the world as a weak and cowardly force, has now become an absolute necessity for the survival of man... We are now faced with the fact, my friends, that tomorrow is today. We are confronted with the fierce urgency of now. In this unfolding *conundrum* of life and history, there is such a thing as being too late."

The final message is from William Faulkner. On December 10th, 1950, his Nobel Prize banquet speech was about the role of humanists in a world facing potential nuclear holocaust.

"I believe that man will not merely endure: he will prevail. He is immortal, not because he alone among creatures has an

阁；我呼吁对全人类包罗一切、无条件的爱。你会因此遭受误解和误读，信奉尼采哲学的世人会认定你是一个软弱和胆怯的懦夫。但是，这却是人类存在下去的绝对必需…… 我的朋友，眼前的事实就是，明天就是今天。此刻，我们正面临最紧急的情况。在变幻莫测的生活和历史中，有一样东西叫作悔之晚矣。"

第二段话引自威廉·福克纳。1950年12月10日，在他的诺贝尔奖获奖晚宴上发表演说中，他谈到了人道主义者在世界核战争的阴影之下应该扮演什么样的角色。

"我相信人类不仅能延续，还会胜利。人是不朽的，不是因为世界万

tribe *n.* 部落
dismiss *v.* 不再考虑；解雇
all-embracing *adj.* 包括一切的；包罗万象的
conundrum *n.* 难题；复杂难解的问题

inexhaustible voice, but because he has a soul, a spirit capable of compassion and sacrifice and endurance. The poet's, the writer's, duty is to write about these things. It is his privilege to help man endure by lifting his heart, by reminding him of the courage and honor and hope and pride and compassion and pity and sacrifice which have been the glory of his past."

Graduates, you have an *extraordinary* role to play in our future. As you pursue your private passions, I hope you will also develop a passion and a voice to help the world in ways both large and small. Nothing will give you greater satisfaction.

Please accept my warmest congratulations. May you *prosper*, may you help preserve and save our planet for your children, and all future children of the world.

物中唯人拥有不倦的声音，而是因为人有灵魂，有能够同情、牺牲和忍耐的精神。而诗人和作家的职责就是书写这些精神。他们有幸通过鼓舞人的斗志，提醒人们牢记昔日荣耀：勇气、荣誉、希望、尊严、同情、怜悯与牺牲精神，以使人类不朽。"

同学们，在我们的未来中，你们将扮演着举足轻重的角色。当你们追求个人的志向时，我希望你们发挥自己的激情，在大大小小各个方面帮助改进这个世界。没有什么比这更能给你们带来满足感了。

最后，请接受我最热烈的祝贺。希望你们获得成功，也希望你们能保护和拯救我们这个星球，为了你们的孩子，以及未来所有的孩子。

---

extraordinary *adj.* 不平常的；非凡的　　　　　　prosper *v.* 兴旺；成功

Speaks at Tsinghua University Ⅰ(Excerpt)

——George Walker Bush

My visit to China comes on an important *anniversary*, as the Vice President mentioned. Thirty years ago this week, an American President arrived in China on a trip designed to end decades of *estrangement* and *confront* centuries of suspicion. President Richard Nixon showed the

清华大学演讲 Ⅰ（节选）

——乔治·沃克·布什

　　我这次访华恰逢一个重要的周年纪念日，正如副主席所提到的，30年前的这一周，一位美国总统来到了中国，他的访华旨在结束两国长达数十年的隔阂，甚至长达数百年的相互猜疑。本着互惠互利、相互尊重的精神，美中两国站在了一起。当尼克松总统离开机场时，周恩来总理对他说了这样一番

anniversary　*n.* 周年纪念（日）
confront　*v.* 遭遇

estrangement　*n.* 疏远；不和

world that two vastly different governments could meet on the grounds of common interest, in the spirit of mutual respect. As they left the airport that day, *Premier* Zhou Enlai said this to President Nixon: "Your handshake *came over* the vastest ocean in the world—25 years of no communication."

During the 30 years since, America and China have exchanged many handshakes of friendship and commerce. And as we have had more contact with each other, the citizens of both countries have gradually learned more about each other. And that's important.

Once America knew China only by its history as a great and enduring civilization. Today, we see a China that is still defined by noble traditions of family, scholarship, and honor. And we see a China that is becoming one of the most *dynamic* and creative societies in the world—as demonstrated by the knowledge and

---

话，他说："你与我的握手越过了世界上最为辽阔的海洋——长达25年的互不交往。"

自那时起，美中两国已经握过多次友谊之手和商业之手。随着我们两国间日益频繁的接触，两国国民对彼此的了解也日益加深，这一点极为重要。

曾经一度，美国人只知道中国拥有悠久的历史和灿烂的文明。如今，我们眼中的中国依然重视家庭、学业和荣誉。同时，我们也看到中国正日益成为世界上一个最富活力和最富创造力的社会之一。在座诸位所具备的知识和潜力便是最好的见证。

---

premier *n.* 总理；首相
dynamic *adj.* 有活力的；有动力的

come over 改变立场；偶然拜访

potential right here in this room.

China is on a rising path, and America welcomes the emergence of a strong and peaceful and prosperous China.

As America learns more about China, I am concerned that the Chinese people do not always see a clear picture of my country. This happens for many reasons, and some of them of our own making. Our movies and television shows often do not *portray* the values of the real America I know.

Our successful businesses show a strength of American commerce, but our spirit, community spirit, and contributions to each other are not always visible as *monetary* success.

In fact, Americans feel a special responsibility for the weak and the poor. Our government spends billions of dollars to provide health care and food and housing for those who cannot help themselves—

中国正在蓬勃发展，而美国欢迎一个强大、和平而又繁荣的中国出现。

当下随着美国人对中国的了解日益加深，我却担心中国人对美国的真实面貌不甚了解。当然，这里面有诸多原因，其中有一些是我们自己造成的。我们的电影和电视节目，往往没有全面反映出我所知道的美国的真正价值观。

我们成功的企业显示了美国商业的力量，金融方面的成功也一目了然，但是我们的精神，我们的团队精神，还有我们对彼此的贡献却难以彰显。

事实上，美国对于保护穷人或弱者有着特殊的责任感，我们政府每年都花费数十亿美元提供医疗、食品和住房保障给那些需要帮助的人。尤为重要

---

portray *v.* 描写；描绘   monetary *adj.* 货币的；金融的

and even more important, many of our citizens contribute their own money and time to help those in need.

American compassion also stretches way beyond our borders. We're the number one provider of humanitarian aid to people in need throughout the world. And as for the men and women of the FBI and law *enforcement*, they're working people; they, themselves, are working people who devote their lives to fighting crime and corruption.

的是，我们的许多公民主动奉献时间、金钱来帮助有需要的人士。

美国人的同情心已经远远地超越了我们自己的国界。在人道主义援助方面，我们居世界首位。至于我们的联邦调查局和执法界人士，他们本身就是劳动人民，而且他们毕生都在致力于打击犯罪和腐败。

enforcement *n.* 实施；执行

21

Speaks at Tsinghua University II(Excerpt)
——George Walker Bush

It was my honor to visit China in 1975—some of you weren't even born then. It shows how old I am. And a lot has changed in your country since then. China has made amazing progress—in openness and enterprise and economic freedom. And this progress previews China's great *potential*.

清华大学演讲 II（节选）
——乔治·沃克·布什

1975年，我曾有幸访华，那时在座的有些同学还没出生，可想而知我现在有多老。从那时起，贵国就发生了翻天覆地的变化，取得了举世闻名的进步，政策开放方面、企业方面、经济自由方面都是如此。从所有这些进步中，我们可以看到中国孕育着巨大的潜力。

potential *n.* 潜力

China has joined the World Trade Organization, and as you *live up to* its obligations, they inevitably will bring changes to China's legal system. A modern China will have a consistent rule of law to govern commerce and secure the rights of its people. The new China your generation is building will need the profound wisdom of your traditions. The *lure* of materialism challenges our society— challenges society in our country, and in many successful countries. Your ancient *ethic* of personal and family responsibility will serve you well.

Behind China's economic success today are talented, brilliant and energetic people. In the near future, those same men and women will play a full and active role in your government. This university is not simply turning out specialists, it is preparing citizens. And citizens are not *spectators* in the affairs of their country. They are participants

中国已经加入了世界贸易组织，在诸位履行义务的同时，贵国的法律制度也发生了相应的变化。一个现代化中国将制定一套完善的法制，来规范其商业活动，保障其人民权力。诸位这一代所建设的新中国需要博大精深的传统智慧，而物质的诱惑既给我们的社会带来挑战，也给我们的国家带来挑战，同时也给世界上很多成功的国家带来挑战。面对这些挑战，重视个人和家庭责任的古老道德传统将使诸位受益匪浅。

推动中国经济取得今天的成功是人才，他们富有智慧而且意气风发。在不久的将来，他们将会在政府中发挥积极、全面的作用，清华大学不仅是培养各领域的专家，也是培育公民的专家。公民在国家事务中不是观众，而是

live up to　遵守；实践　　　　　　　　　　lure *n.* 吸引；引诱
ethic *n.* 道德（行为）准则　　　　　　　spectator *n.* 观众；旁观者

in its future.

Change is coming. China is already having secret *ballot* and competitive elections at the local level. Nearly 20 years ago, a great Chinese leader, Deng Xiaoping, said this—I want you to hear his words. He said that China would eventually expand *democratic* elections all the way to the national level. I look forward to that day.

All these changes will lead to a stronger, more confident China—a China that can astonish and enrich the world, a China that your *generation* will help create. This is one of the most exciting times in the history of your country, a time when even the grandest hopes seem within your reach.

My nation offers you our respect and our friendship. Six years

---

未来的建设者。

变革正在到来，中国已经在地方实行不计名投票和差额选举。大概是20年前，中国伟大的领导人邓小平曾说中国最终会将民主选举推广到全国范围。我期待着这一天的到来。

所有这些变化都会让中国变得更强大，更自信，这样的中国使世界瞩目，也令世界更加丰富多彩，而这样的中国要靠你们来创造。现在中国正处在一个历史上非常令人振奋的时刻，此时此刻，最宏伟的梦想也似乎唾手可得。

对此，美国向贵国致以敬意，并伸出友谊之手。再过6年，来自美国和

---

ballot *n.* 投票   democratic *adj.* 民主的
generation *n.* 一代人

from now, athletes from America and around the world will come to your country for the Olympic games. And I'm confident they will find a China that is becoming a daguo, a leading nation, at peace with its people and at peace with the world.

Thank you for letting me come.

全世界的运动员们将到贵国参加奥运会。我坚信，他们见到的中国将是一个正在崛起的大国，一个走在世界前沿，与其人民无争，与世界和平相处的中国。

最后谢谢诸位让我到此演讲。

Inequity and Complexity of the Word Ⅰ(Excerpt)

Bill Gates 2007 Harvard Commencement Speech

What I remember above all about Harvard was being *in the midst of* so much energy and intelligence. It could be *exhilarating*, *intimidating*, sometimes even discouraging, but always challenging. It was an amazing privilege—and though I left early, I was

世界之不平等与复杂性 Ⅰ（节选）

比尔·盖茨2007年在哈佛毕业典礼上的演讲

在我的记忆中，哈佛充满青春活力，而且人才辈出。哈佛的生活既令人愉快，也让人感到压力，有时甚至会让人泄气，但永远都充满挑战。生活在哈佛是极大的荣幸……虽然我离开得比较早，但我在这里的经历、在这里结识的朋友及在这里产生的一些想法影响了我一生。

---

in the midst of 在……之中；正当……的时候　　　　exhilarating *adj.* 使人兴奋的
intimidating *adj.* 威胁的；咄咄逼人的

transformed by my years at Harvard, the friendships I made, and the ideas I worked on.

But taking a serious look back ... I do have one big regret.

I left Harvard with no real awareness of the awful inequities in the world—the *appalling disparities* of health, and wealth, and opportunity that *condemn* millions of people to lives of despair.

I learned a lot here at Harvard about new ideas in economics and politics. I got great exposure to the advances being made in the sciences.

But humanity's greatest advances are not in its discoveries—but in how those discoveries are applied to reduce inequity. Whether through *democracy*, strong public education, quality health care, or broad economic opportunity—reducing inequity is the highest human achievement.

但是，仔细回想过去，我确实有一大遗憾。

我离开哈佛时，根本没有意识到这个世界是多么不平等。人类在健康、财富和机遇上的不平等大得可怕，被迫使得无数人在绝望中生活。

我在哈佛学到了很多经济学和政治学的新思想，也了解到了很多科学上的新进展。

但是，人类最大的进步并不是这些发现，而是如何用这些发现去减少那些不平等现象。不管通过何种手段——建立民主制度、健全公共教育体系、提高医疗保健制度、还是创造广泛的经济机会——减少不平等始终是人类最大的成就。

---

appalling *adj.* 骇人的；可怕的　　　　disparity *n.* 不同；差异
condemn *v.* 使陷入（不愉快的境地）　　democracy *n.* 民主；民主制；民主国家

I left campus knowing little about the millions of young people cheated out of educational opportunities here in this country. And I knew nothing about the millions of people living in *unspeakable* poverty and disease in developing countries.

It took me decades to find out.

You graduates came to Harvard at a different time. You know more about the world's inequities than the classes that came before. In your years here, I hope you've had a chance to think about how— in this age of *accelerating* technology—we can finally take on these inequities, and we can solve them.

Imagine, just for the sake of discussion, that you had a few hours a week and a few dollars a month to donate to a cause—and

---

我离开校园的时候，根本不知道在这个国家里，还有数百万年轻人无力获得受教育的机会。我也不知道，在发展中国家，还有无数人生活在让人无法形容的贫穷和疾病之中。

几十年后我才明白了这些事情。

在座的各位同学，你们来到哈佛的时代与我不同。你们应该比以前的学生更了解这个世界的不平等。我希望你们在哈佛求学的过程中曾思考过这样一个问题，那就是在这个新技术加速发展的时代，我们最终该怎样应对这种不平等并解决这个问题。

为了方便讨论，请想象一下，假如你每个星期都可以匀出一些时间、每

---

unspeakable *adj.* 不能以言语表达的   accelerate *v.* （使）加快，（使）增速

you wanted to spend that time and money where it would have the greatest impact in saving and improving lives. Where would you spend it?

For Melinda and for me, the challenge is the same: how can we do the most good for the greatest number with the resources we have.

During our discussions on this question, Melinda and I read an article about the millions of children who were dying every year in poor countries from diseases that we had long ago made harmless in this country. Measles, *malaria*, *pneumonia*, *hepatitis* B, yellow fever. One disease I had never even heard of, rotavirus, was killing half a million kids each year—none of them in the United States.

个月都可以捐出一些钱，如果可以将这些时间和金钱用到对拯救生命和改善人类生活最有用的地方的话，你会选择什么地方？

这也是我和梅琳达面临的问题：如何让我们拥有的资源发挥最大的作用。

在讨论的过程中，我和梅琳达读到一篇文章，里面讲在那些贫穷的国家，每年都有数百万的儿童死于那些在美国早已能够治愈的疾病——麻疹、疟疾、肺炎、乙型肝炎、黄热病，还有一种以前我从未听说过的轮状病毒。这些疾病每年会导致50万儿童死亡，但是在美国这类死亡病例一例也没有。

---

malaria *n.* 疟疾   pneumonia *n.* 肺炎
hepatitis *n.* 肝炎

We were shocked. We had just assumed that if millions of children were dying and they could be saved, the world would make it a priority to discover and deliver the medicines to save them. But it did not. For under a dollar, there were *interventions* that could save lives that just weren't being delivered.

If you believe that every life has equal value, it's *revolting to* learn that some lives are seen as worth saving and others are not. We said to ourselves: "This can't be true. But if it is true, it deserves to be the priority of our giving."

So we began our work in the same way anyone here would begin it. We asked: "How could the world let these children die?"

The answer is simple, and harsh. The market did not reward

我们震惊了。我们想，如果几百万可以获救的儿童正挣扎在死亡线上，那么这个世界理应将用药物拯救他们作为头等大事。但事实却并非如此。仅因为不足一美元的资金问题而受到干涉，这些药物并没有送到他们的手中。

如果你相信每个生命都是平等的，那么当你发现有人认为某些生命值得救助，而另一些生命不值得时，你会深感厌恶。我们对自己说："事情不可能如此。如果真是如此，那么这理应是我们努力的头等大事。"

所以，我们可以用任何人都会想到的方式开始工作。我们问："这个世界怎么可以眼睁睁看着这些孩子死去？"

答案很简单，也很令人难堪。在市场经济中，拯救儿童是一项没有利润

---

intervention *n.* 介入；干涉；干预　　　　　　　revolt to 起义；反叛

saving the lives of these children, and governments did not *subsidize* it. So the children died because their mothers and their fathers had no power in the market and no voice in the system.

But you and I have both.

We can make market forces work better for the poor if we can develop a more creative capitalism—if we can stretch the reach of market forces so that more people can make a profit, or at least make a living, serving people who are *suffering from* the worst inequities. We also can press governments around the world to spend taxpayer money in ways that better reflect the values of the people who pay the taxes.

的工作，而且政府也不会提供补助。这些儿童之所以会死亡，是因为他们的父母既没有经济实力也没有政治权力。

但是，你们和我都有！

如果我们能够让资本主义制度更具创造力，我们就可以让市场更好地服务穷人——如果我们可以改变市场，让更多人获利，或者至少可以维持生活——那么，我们就可以帮到那些正在极端不平等的境况中受苦的人们。我们还可以向全世界的政府施压，要求他们将纳税人的钱，花到更能反映纳税人价值的地方去。

---

subsidize *v.* 资助；补助；给······发津贴   suffer from   遭受；因······而蒙受损害

23

Inequity and Complexity of the Word II(Excerpt)

Bill Gates 2007 Harvard Commencement Speech

Should our best minds *be dedicated to* solving our biggest problems?

Should Harvard encourage its *faculty* to take on the world's worst inequities? Should Harvard students learn about the depth of global poverty... the *prevalence* of world hunger... the *scarcity*

世界之不平等与复杂性 II（节选）

比尔·盖茨2007年在哈佛毕业典礼上的演讲

我们最优秀的人才是否在致力于解决我们最大的问题？

哈佛是否应鼓励其教师去解决世界上最严重的不平等问题？哈佛的学生是否了解全球性的贫困？……是否了解世界性的饥荒？……是否了解清洁水资源的匮乏？……是否了解失学女童？……是否了解那些死于非恶性疾病的

---

be dedicated to　从事于；致力于
prevalence　n. 传播；流行；普及

faculty　n. 全体教员；能力；天赋
scarcity　n. 缺乏；不足；稀少

of clean water... the girls kept out of school... the children who die from diseases we can cure?

Should the world's most privileged people learn about the lives of the world's least privileged?

These are not *rhetorical* questions— you will answer with your policies.

My mother, who was filled with pride the day I was admitted here—never stopped *pressing me to do* more for others. A few days before my wedding, she hosted a *bridal* event, at which she read aloud a letter about marriage that she had written to Melinda. My mother was very ill with cancer at the time, but she saw one more opportunity to deliver her message, and at the close of the letter she said: "From those to whom much is given, much is expected."

When you consider what those of us here in this Yard have been

---

儿童？

世界上那些养尊处优的人们，你们是否了解那些生活贫困的人们？

这不是反问，是想让你们用行动来回答。

我收到哈佛大学录取通知那天，我母亲非常自豪，但她一直敦促我，要为他人谋取更多的福祉。在我结婚的前几天，她特意主持了一个仪式。在这个仪式上，她高声朗读了一封关于解决婚姻方面问题的信，是写给梅林达的。那时，我母亲身患癌症，而且已病入膏肓，但她还是抓住了一线机会，传播她的信念。在那封信的结尾，她写道："得到越多，期望越大。"

在座各位，请想一想，你们得到了什么——天赋、特权、机遇——既然

---

rhetorical *adj.* 反问的
bridal *adj.* 婚礼（的）

press sb. to do sth. 强迫某人做某事

given in talent, privilege, and opportunity there is almost no limit to what the world has a right to expect from us.

In line with the promise of this age, I want to *exhort* each of the graduates here to take on an issue a complex problem, a deep inequity, and become a specialist on it. If you make it the focus of your career that would be *phenomenal*. But you don't have to do that to make an impact. For a few hours every week, you can use the growing power of the Internet to get informed, find others with the same interests, see the *barriers*, and find ways to *cut through* them.

Don't let complexity stop you. Be activists. Take on the big inequities. It will be one of the great experiences of your lives.

You graduates are coming of age in an amazing time. As you leave Harvard, you have technology that members of my class

如此，全世界的人都在期望，期望我们为整个世界做出无穷无尽的贡献。

同时代的期望一样，我也要鼓励在座各位毕业生去解决一个问题，一个复杂的问题，一个深刻的社会不平等问题，然后把自己变成这方面的专家。如果你们能够以此作为你们的职业目标，你们将会脱颖而出。但是，你不可以为了扩大影响而做。只要一星期花几个小时，你就可以从日益壮大的互联网上获得信息，找到志同道合的朋友，发现困难所在，并找到解决困难的途径。

不要让这个复杂的社会阻碍你前进的步伐。要做一个行动主义者。将解决人类的不平等视为己任，这会成为你生命中最伟大的经历。

在座的各位毕业生们，你们所处的时代是一个神奇的时代。当你们离开

exhort　*v.* 力劝；勉励　　　　　　　phenomenal　*adj.* 非凡的；出众的
barrier　*n.* 栅栏；关卡；障碍　　　　cut through　克服；穿透

never had. You have awareness of global inequity, which we did not have. And with that awareness, you likely also have an informed conscience that will *torment* you if you abandon these people whose lives you could change with very little effort. You have more than we had; you must start sooner, and carry on longer. Knowing what you know, how could you not?

And I hope you will come back here to Harvard 30 years from now and reflect on what you have done with your talent and your energy. I hope you will judge yourselves not on your professional accomplishments alone, but also on how well you have addressed the world's deepest inequities... on how well you treated people a world away who have nothing in common with you but their humanity.

哈佛的时候，你们所拥有的技术是我们那时不曾拥有的，你们了解到的社会不平等现象也是我们那时不曾了解的。认识到了这个问题后，如果你弃之不顾，你可能会受到良心的谴责，因此只需要一点小小的努力，你就可以改变那些人的生活。你们比我们拥有更大的能力，所以你们应该尽早开始这项事业，并坚持不懈地做下去。既然了解了这一切，你们怎么还能无动于衷呢？

我希望，30 年后你们再回到哈佛时，可以回想起你们用自己青春才智所做出的一切。我希望，在那个时候，你们用来评价自己的标准，不仅仅是你们的学业成就，还包括你们为改变社会不平等所做出的努力，以及你们如何善待那些远隔千山万水的人们，尽管他们与你们毫不相关，但有一个相通的共同点就是同为人类。

---

torment *v.* 折磨

Commencement Address at Harvard University(Excerpt)

—— Mary Robinson

...

I'm proud to see so many capable young men and women about to *embark on* a future career where they can put their years of learning and preparation to good use. Having passed through the *rigors* of a formal education, you are now ready to assume new

哈佛大学毕业典礼上的演讲（节选）

——玛丽·罗宾逊

......

看到这么多能力显著的年轻人即将把多年所学投入到未来的事业中，我感到骄傲。经过正规教育的严格洗礼，你们将为承担新的责任与任务而整装待发，将在一个充满机遇的世界里，用你们的成绩、你们的博爱以及你们准

---

embark on　从事；着手

rigor　*n.* 严峻

responsibilities and tasks, becoming answerable only to yourselves with regards to your performance, your humanity and your *soundness* of judgement, in a world full of possibilities.

But I would ask you to remember that it's not a world full of possibilities for all. Each of you has been the *beneficiary* of a rare privilege. You have received an exceptional education at an exceptional place when there are many, in both your country and mine, and in many, many other parts of our world, who are just as *innately* talented and just as ambitious as you are but will never have such an opportunity. I say this not to make you feel guilty. You should be proud of what you have achieved. But I do ask that you

---

确的判断力书写人生的答卷。

但请你们记住，并非世界上所有人都有这种机会。但在座各位都已获此殊荣。你们在这所举世闻名的学府接受最好的教育，而同时在你我的国家及世界上许多其他地方，有很多人像你们一样有天赋，一样有雄心壮志，但却永远不会有这样的机会。我这样说不是为了要让你们深感内疚，你们理应为自己取得的成绩备感自豪。但我诚挚地恳请大家把所学知识用在最值得追求

---

soundness *n.* 健康；完好　　beneficiary *n.* 受惠者；（遗产的）受益人
innately *adv.* 天生就有地

use your education to pursue only the worthiest of goals; goals that contribute to the *betterment* of the lives of others; and goals that give you personal satisfaction because of their contribution to the society we live in.

You who graduate today, and you who are recent and not so recent graduates, who return to meet your Harvard friends again, can, I believe, do much to contribute to the betterment of society. You can become interested and involved in the world around you. *By virtue of* your education, you can offer society the benefit of your focused knowledge, as well as a wider vision and a great sense of purpose. You also have the skills to teach others to be more tolerant,

---

的目标上；致力于给他人创造更美好的生活；致力于为我们的社会做出更大的贡献。

在座诸位毕业生们，毕业后回来与哈佛再聚的同学们，老毕业生们，我相信，你们一定会为创造更美好的社会而做出更多贡献。你们会对身边的世界更感兴趣、更投入。你们所接受的教育让你们可以用所学的专业知识、广博的智慧和一种庄严的使命感来造福社会。你们有本领教会他人更多宽容、

---

betterment *n.* 改进；改良　　　　　　　by virtue of　借助；由于

more understanding and more caring, and I'm confident that your recognition of this special responsibility will guide your actions and perhaps one day—and I think I saw some potential candidates—inspire a future Eleanor Roosevelt.

I wish you much happiness and success in the years ahead. May your memories of Harvard, as mine are, and the friends you have made here be with you always. Congratulations, new graduates, and I am very honored to be linked with the honored graduates up here of 1998 and to be *rejuvenated* by joining the class of 1998. Thank you very much.

更多理解和关怀，我相信，一旦你们认识到这份特殊的责任，它就会引导你们行动。也许有一天，我想我会看到一些未来的候选人，未来的爱莲娜·罗斯福出现。

最后，祝你们今后生活幸福、事业成功。愿哈佛留给你们的记忆像我一样美好，愿你们和在这儿结交的朋友友谊长存。恭喜你们，新毕业生们，能与98届毕业生们在一起，成为这集体的一员，我深感荣幸，这也让我备感年轻。谢谢你们！

rejuvenate *v.* 恢复活力

25

Address at the Democratic National Convention Ⅰ
—— Barack Hussein Obama

On behalf of the great state of *Illinois*, *crossroads* of a nation, land of Lincoln, let me express my deep gratitude for the privilege of addressing this *convention*. Tonight is a particular honor for me because, let's face it, my presence on this stage is pretty unlikely. My father was a foreign student, born

民主党大会上的演讲 Ⅰ
——巴拉克·侯赛因·奥巴马

　　伟大的伊利诺伊州既是全国的交通枢纽，也是林肯的故乡，作为州代表，我很荣幸今天有机会在大会上致辞。今晚对我而言非同寻常，不得不承认，我能站在这里本身就已意义非凡。我父亲是个外国留学生，他生于肯尼亚的一个小村庄，并在那里长大成人。他小时候放过羊，读书的学校也简陋

Illinois *n.* 伊利诺伊州（美国州名）　　　　crossroad *n.* 交叉路口；十字路

convention *n.* 会议；习俗

and raised in a small village in Kenya. He grew up herding goats, went to school in a tin-roof shack. His father, my grandfather, was a cook, a domestic servant.

But my grandfather had larger dreams for his son. Through hard work and *perseverance* my father got a scholarship to study in a magical place: America, which stood as a *beacon* of freedom and opportunity to so many who had come before. While studying here, my father met my mother. She was born in a town on the other side of the world, in Kansas. Her father worked on *oil rigs* and farms through most of the Depression. The day after Pearl Harbor he signed up for duty, joined Patton's army and marched across Europe. Back home, my grandmother raised their baby and went to work on a bomber *assembly* line. After the war, they studied on the GI Bill, bought a house through FHA, and moved west in search of

---

不堪，屋顶上仅有块铁皮来遮风挡雨。而他的父亲，我的祖父，不过是个普通的厨子，而且还做过家佣。

但祖父对父亲寄予了厚望。凭借坚持不懈的努力和坚韧不拔的毅力，父亲拿到了奖学金，并赴美留学。对于很多踏上这片国土的人而言，美国这片神奇的土地，意味着自由和机遇。在留学期间，我的父亲与母亲不期而遇。母亲来自一个与父亲完全不同的世界，她生于堪萨斯的一个小镇。大萧条时期，外祖父为谋生计，曾在石油钻塔打过工，也在农场务过农。日军偷袭珍珠港后第二天，他自愿应征入伍，随巴顿将军转战南北，横扫欧洲。在后方的家中，外祖母在轰炸机装配线上找了份生活，含辛茹苦，抚育子女。战后，依据士兵福利法案，他们通过联邦住宅管理局购置了一套房子，并举家西

---

perseverance *n.* 坚毅

oil rig 石油钻塔

beacon *n.* 信号灯；闪光灯

assembly *n.* 组装；议会；集会

opportunity.

And they, too, had big dreams for their daughter, a common dream, born of two continents. My parents shared not only an improbable love; they shared an *abiding* faith in the possibilities of this nation. They would give me an African name, Barack, or "blessed", believing that in a tolerant America your name is no barrier to success. They imagined me going to the best schools in the land, even though they weren't rich, because in a generous America you don't have to be rich to achieve your potential. They are both passed away now. Yet, I know that, on this night, they look down on me with pride.

I stand here today, grateful for the *diversity* of my *heritage*, aware that my parents' dreams live on in my precious daughters. I stand here knowing that my story is part of the larger American story, that I

迁，以期望谋求更大发展。

对自己的女儿，外祖父也寄予厚望，虽然出生在非洲和美洲两个不同的大陆，但两家人却有着共同的梦想。我的父母不仅不可思议地相爱了，而且还对这个国家有了坚定不移的信念。他们赐予我一个非洲名字，巴拉克，意为"上天福佑"，因为他们相信，在这个如此包容的国度中，这样的名字不会成为成功的羁绊。尽管生活并不宽裕，他们还是想方设法让我接受当地最好的教育。在这样一个富足的国度，无论贫富贵贱，都给人同样的机会发展个人的潜力。虽然现在他们都已过世，不过，我知道，此时此刻他们在天之灵，正在骄傲地注视着我。

今天，站在这里，我对自己身上这种特殊的血统而心怀感激，我知道

---

abiding *adj.* 持久不变的；永久的   diversity *n.* 多样；变化万千
heritage *n.* 遗产；继承物

owe a debt to all of those who came before me, and that, in no other country on earth, is my story even possible. Tonight, we gather to affirm the greatness of our nation, not because of the height of our *skyscrapers*, or the power of our military, or the size of our economy. Our pride is based on a very simple *premise*, summed up in a declaration made over two hundred years ago, "We hold these truths to be self-evident, that all men are created equal. That they are *endowed* by their Creator with certain *inalienable* rights. That among these are life, liberty and the pursuit of happiness."

父母的梦想将在我的宝贝女儿身上延续。站在这里，我深知自己的经历只是千百万美国故事中的沧海一粟，更深知自己无法忘却那些更早踏上这片土地的先人，因为若不是在美国，我的故事无论如何都不可能发生。今夜，我们聚集一堂，再次证明这个国度的伟大，这一切并不在于鳞次栉比的摩天大厦，也不在于傲视群雄的军备实力，更不在于稳健雄厚的经济实力。我们的自豪与荣耀来自一个非常简单的前提，两百多年前，它在一个著名的宣言中得以高度的概括："我们认为以下真理不言而喻，人生来平等，造物主赐予他们这些不可剥夺的权利：生命、自由和对幸福的追求。"

skyscraper *n.* 摩天大楼
endow *v.* 给予；赋予

premise *n.* 前提
inalienable *adj.* 不可剥夺的

Address at the Democratic National Convention II

—— Barack Hussein Obama

That is the true genius of America, a faith in the simple dreams of its people, the insistence on small miracles. That we can *tuck in* our children at night and know they are fed and clothed and safe from harm. That we can say what we think, write what we think, without hearing a sudden knock on the door.

民主党大会上的演讲 Ⅱ

——巴拉克·侯赛因·奥巴马

这才是真正的美国智慧，坚信自己的国民有着朴实的梦想，坚信点滴的奇迹终会发生。入夜，我们为孩子掖好被子，相信他们将来不会为衣食所忧，为安全所困。我们可以畅所欲言，无须担心不速之客不请自来。我们有灵感，有想法，可以去实现，去创业，无须行贿或以雇佣某些人物的子女作

tuck in　给……盖好被子；痛快地吃

That we can have an idea and start our own business without paying a bribe or hiring somebody's son. That we can participate in the political process without fear of *retribution*, and that our votes will he counted—or at least, most of the time.

This year, in this election, we are called to reaffirm our values and commitments, to hold them against a hard reality and see how we are measuring up, to the *legacy* of our forbearers, and the promise of future generations. And fellow Americans—Democrats, Republicans, Independents—I say to you tonight: we have more work to do. More to do for the workers I met in Galesburg, Illinois, who are losing their union jobs at the Maytag plant that's moving to Mexico, and now are having to compete with their own children for jobs that pay seven bucks an hour. More to do for the father I met who was losing his job and choking back tears, wondering how he would pay $4,500

为筹码和条件。我们可以参政议政，不必担心打击报复，多数情况下，我们的选票能起到举足轻重的作用。

今年的选举特别重申了我们所拥有的价值观和肩负的责任，以此应对当下的艰难世道，学会怎样更好地秉承前辈的遗产，实现对子孙的承诺。诸位美国公民，无论你是民主党人，共和党人，还是无党派人士，今晚我想对大家说的是：我们要做的事情还有很多。在伊利诺伊州盖尔斯伯格，由于梅塔格公司要迁至墨西哥，很多工人将面临失业，不得不和自己的子女一起竞争每小时 7 美元的低薪工作。我曾遇到过一位父亲，他丢了工作，强忍着泪水，不知怎样才能支付得起儿子每月4，500 美元的高昂医药费用，本可救命

retribution *n.* 报应；罚　　　　　legacy *n.* 遗赠的财物；遗产

a month for the drugs his son needs without the health benefits he *counted on*. More to do for the young woman in East St. Louis, and thousands more like her, who has the grades, has the drive, has the will, but doesn't have the money to go to college.

Don't get me wrong. The people I meet in small towns and big cities, in diners and office parks, they don't expect government to solve all their problems. They know they have to work hard to get ahead and they want to. Go into the collar counties around Chicago, and people will tell you they don't want their tax money wasted by a welfare agency or the *Pentagon*. Go into any inner city neighborhood, and folks will tell you that government alone can't teach kids to learn. They know that parents have to parent, that children can't achieve unless we raise their expectations and turn off the television sets and *eradicate* the *slander* that says a black youth with a book is acting white.

的医疗保险对他而言却遥不可及。对他们，我们应该做点什么？在东圣路易斯市，有这样一个年轻女孩，她品学兼优，坚忍不拔，却没钱上大学，而像她这样的孩子还有千千万万。对于她们，我们又该做点什么？

请正面理解我的意思。在城市或乡镇，餐厅或办公楼停车场，我接触过很多民众，他们并不期待政府出面帮他们排忧解难。而是清楚地意识到，他们需要通过自身努力，去面对和解决所有问题。走进芝加哥周边的城镇，大家会告诉你，希望自己辛苦缴纳的税款能够物尽其用，而不是让社会保障机构或国防机构任意支配；走进市中心的街区，大家会告诉你，让孩子好好读书不能仅依靠政府的力量，父母尽职尽责，培养下一代，不要让孩子整天沉溺于电视；对于黑人而言，更要和白人一样，拥有同样受教育的权利。人们

---

count on 依靠；指望　　　　　　　Pentagon 五角大楼（美国国防部）
eradicate v. 根除　　　　　　　　slander n. 诽谤

No, people don't expect government to solve all their problems. But they sense, deep in their bones, that with just a change in priorities, we can make sure that every child in America has a decent shot at life, and that the doors of opportunity remain open to all. They know we can do better. And they want that choice.

In this election, we offer that choice. Our party has chosen a man to lead us who embodies the best this country has to offer. That man is John Kerry. John Kerry understands the ideals of community, faith, and sacrifice, because they've defined his life. From his heroic service in Vietnam to his years as *prosecutor* and *lieutenant* governor, through two decades in the United States *Senate*, he has devoted himself to this country. Again and again, we've seen him make tough choices when easier ones were available. His values and his record affirm what is best in us.

并非想依赖政府来解决所有问题，他们真挚地认为，只要政府把工作重心调整一下，就可以让每个孩子都能奋发图强，让机遇大门向每个人都敞开。他们深知，我们有能力做得更好，他们也希望我们能做得更好。

在本次选举中，我们已做出了选择。民主党已选出一名最优秀的人士作为我们的领袖，带领大家实现这样的愿望。他就是约翰·克里，他深刻地领悟了社会、信仰和献身精神这样崇高的理想，因为这些铸就了他生命的全部。他曾在越南战争中英勇作战，回国后担任过检察官和副州长，在美国参议院度过了20个春秋，把全部精力都投入到国家的社稷大业之中。多少次，面对艰难抉择时，他知难而上，不畏艰险，他的阅历和品行为我们树立了榜样。

---

prosecutor *n.* 起诉人   lieutenant *n.* 陆军中尉；海军上尉

senate *n.* 参议院；上院

27

Address at the Democratic National Convention III

—— Barack Hussein Obama

Yet even as we speak, there are those who are preparing to divide us, the spin masters and negative ad *peddlers* who embrace the politics of anything goes. Well, I say to them tonight, there's not a liberal America and a *conservative* America—there's the United States of America. There's

---

民主党大会上的演讲 Ⅲ
——巴拉克·侯赛因·奥巴马

　　甚至我们在这里聚会之时，那些操纵舆论、制作负面宣传并投身于没有原则和不择手段的政治的人还准备分裂我们。今晚，我要告诉这些人，没有所谓的自由派美国和保守派美国之分，只有一个美利坚合众国。也没有所谓的白人和黑人之分，更没有拉丁裔和亚裔之分，有的只是美利坚合众国国

---

peddler *n.* 宣扬者；散布者　　　　　　　conservative *adj.* 保守的；传统的

not a black America and white America and Latino America and Asian America; there's the United States of America. The *pundits* like to slice-and-dice our country into Red States and Blue States; Red States for Republicans, Blue States for Democrats. But I've got news for them, too. We worship an awesome God in the Blue States, and we don't like federal agents poking around our libraries in the Red States. We coach Little League in the Blue States and have gay friends in the Red States. There are *patriots* who opposed the war in Iraq and patriots who supported it. We are one people, all of us pledging *allegiance* to the stars and stripes, all of us defending the United States of America.

民。有人想将我们国家分成红蓝两色，红色代表共和党，蓝色代表民主党。但我想说，在民主党中，我们也都信奉万能的主，我们不希望联邦特工在共和党中间对我们的藏书指指点点。我们民主党中也有人执教少年棒球联盟，而在共和党中也有同性恋朋友，既有爱国人士支持伊拉克战争，也有爱国人士反对就伊出兵。我们都是一国之民，都效忠于伟大的星条旗，都热爱我们的祖国——美利坚合众国。

pundit *n.* 权威人士；专家

patriot *n.* 爱国者；爱国主义者

allegiance *n.* 忠诚

In the end, that's what this election is about. Do we participate in a politics of *cynicism* or a politics of hope? John Kerry calls on us to hope. John Edwards calls on us to hope. I'm not talking about blind optimism here—the almost willful ignorance that thinks unemployment will go away if we just don't talk about it, or the health care crisis will solve itself if we just ignore it. No, I'm talking about something more substantial. It's the hope of slaves sitting around a fire singing freedom songs; the hope of immigrants setting out for distant shores; the hope of a young naval *lieutenant* bravely *patrolling* the Mekong Delta; the hope of a millworker's son who dares to *defy* the odds; the hope of a skinny kid with a funny name who believes that America has a place for him, too. The audacity of hope!

　　说到底，这才是本次选举的意义所在：我们所参与的政治应该是愤世嫉俗还是充满希望？约翰·克里号召我们要对未来满怀希望，约翰·爱德华兹也号召我们要对未来充满希望。这并非说我们要盲目乐观，认为只要不谈论失业问题，失业就会自行消失；认为无视医疗危机，它就会自行解决。我所谈的是更实质的问题。是奴隶们围坐在火堆边，吟唱自由之歌所怀的希望；是人们远涉重洋，移民他乡所怀有的希望；是年轻的海军上尉在湄公河三角洲勇敢的巡逻放哨时怀有的希望；是出身工人家庭的孩子勇敢挑战自己命运时的希望；是我这个名字怪怪的瘦小子相信美国这片热土有自己容身之地时所拥有的希望。这就是无畏的希望。

---

cynicism　*n.* 愤世嫉俗　　　　　　　lieutenant　*n.* 陆军中尉；海军上尉
patrol　*v.* 巡逻；巡查　　　　　　　defy　*v.* 不服从；反抗

In the end, that is God's greatest gift to us, the bedrock of this nation; the belief in things not seen; the belief that there are better days ahead. I believe we can give our middle class relief and provide working families with a road to opportunity. I believe we can provide jobs to the jobless, homes to the homeless, and reclaim young people in cities across America from violence and despair. I believe that as we stand on the crossroads of history, we can make the right choices, and meet the challenges that face us America!

Tonight, if you feel the same energy I do, the same urgency I do, the same *passion* I do, the same hopefulness I do—if we do what we must do, then I have no doubt that all across the country, from

最后，感谢上苍赐予我们这个最好的礼物，这也是我们国家赖以生存的基石。我们相信最好的东西尚未出现，相信更好的日子就在明天。我相信我们可以为中产阶级减负，让工人家庭走上希望之路。我相信我们可以为无业者创造就业机会，为无家可归者提供遮风挡雨的港湾，让美国城市中的年轻人从暴力和绝望的阴影中走出来。我相信今天的我们就站在历史的十字街头，我们可以做出正确抉择，直面挑战。

今晚，如果你我感同身受，有同样的力量、同样的迫切感、同样的激情和同样的希望；如果我们都能行动起来，那么我相信，从佛罗里达到俄勒

passion *n.* 激情

Florida to Oregon, from Washington to Maine, the people will rise up in November, and John Kerry will be sworn in as president, and John Edwards will be sworn in as vice president, and this country will reclaim its promise, and out of this long political darkness a brighter day will come. Thank you and God bless you.

冈，从华盛顿到缅因州，在11月积极行动起来，使得约翰·克里、约翰·爱德华兹分别宣誓就任总统、副总统之职，国家也将就此走出低谷、重整旗鼓。暗夜即将过去，黎明即将到来。谢谢大家，愿上帝保佑你们！

We Are What We Choose I

Remarks by Jeff Bezos, as Delivered to the Class of 2010,
Baccalaureate Princeton University

As a kid, I spent my summers with my grandparents on their *ranch* in Texas. I helped fix *windmills*, *vaccinate* cattle, and do other chores. We also watched soap operas every afternoon, especially *"Days of our Lives."* My grandparents belonged to a *Caravan* Club, a group of Airstream trailer

---

决定成就我们 I

杰夫·贝佐斯在普林斯顿大学 2010 年毕业典礼上的讲话

小时候，夏天我总是会待在德州祖父母的农场中。我帮他们修理风车，为牛接种疫苗，以及做其他杂事。每天下午，我们都一起看肥皂剧，尤其是《我们的岁月》。我祖父母参加了一个由一群驾驶福特概念车的人

---

ranch *n.* 大牧场；饲养场   windmill *n.* 风车

vaccinate *v.* 接种疫苗   caravan *n.* 旅行拖车；大篷车

owners who travel together around the U.S. and Canada. And every few summers, we'd join the caravan. We'd hitch up the Airstream trailer to my grandfather's car, and off we'd go, in a line with 300 other Airstream adventurers.

I loved and worshipped my grandparents and I really looked forward to these trips. On one particular trip, I was about 10 years old. I was rolling around in the big bench seat in the back of the car. My grandfather was driving. And my grandmother had the passenger seat. She smoked throughout these trips, and I hated the smell.

At that age, I'd take any excuse to make estimates and do minor *arithmetic*. I'd calculate our gas *mileage*—figure out useless statistics on things like grocery spending. I'd been hearing an ad campaign about smoking. I can't remember the details, but basically the ad said, every *puff* of a cigarette takes some number of minutes off of your life: I think it might have been two minutes per puff. At any

---

们组成的房车俱乐部，他们打算结伴游遍美国和加拿大。每隔几个夏天，我也会加入他们。我们把房车挂在祖父的小汽车后面，然后加入到由300余名房车探险者们组成的浩荡队伍中。

我爱我的祖父母，也崇拜他们，真心期盼每一次旅行。记得我10岁那年的一次旅行，我照例坐在后座的长椅上，祖父开着车，祖母坐在他旁边，吸着烟。我讨厌烟味。

在那样的年纪，我会找各种借口做些估算或者小算术。我会计算油耗或者杂货花销这类鸡毛蒜皮的小事。我听过一个有关吸烟的广告，但具体细节不记得了，只记得广告大意是，每吸一口香烟会减少几分钟的寿命什

---

arithmetic *n.* 算术

puff *v.* （抽）一口烟；喘息

mileage *n.* 里程；英里数

rate, I decided to do the math for my grandmother. I estimated the number of cigarettes per day, estimated the number of puffs per cigarette and so on. When I was satisfied that I'd come up with a reasonable number, I poked my head into the front of the car, tapped my grandmother on the shoulder, and proudly *proclaimed*, "At two minutes per puff, you've taken nine years off your life!"

I have a vivid memory of what happened, and it was not what I expected. I expected to be applauded for my cleverness and arithmetic skills. "Jeff, you're so smart. You had to have made some tricky estimates, figure out the number of minutes in a year and do some division." That's not what happened. Instead, my grandmother burst into tears. I sat in the backseat and did not know what to do. While my grandmother sat crying, my grandfather, who had been driving in silence, pulled over onto the shoulder of the highway. He got out of the car and came around and opened my door and

么的，大概是两分钟吧。无论如何，我决定为祖母算算。我估算出祖母每天要吸几支香烟，每支香烟要吸几口等等，然后心满意足地得出了一个合理的数字。接着，我捅了捅坐在前面的祖母，拍了拍她的肩膀，骄傲地宣称，"你每天吸两分钟的烟，就会少活9年!"

我清晰地记得接下来所发生的事，结果有些出乎我的意料。我本期待着我的小聪明和算术技巧能赢来掌声，但结果并非如此。相反，我的祖母哭了起来。祖父之前一直在默默开车，后来他把车停在路边，走下车来，打开了我的车门，等着我跟他下车。我惹麻烦了吗？我的祖父是一个聪明而安静的人。他从来没有对我说过严厉的话，难道这会是第一次？还是他

proclaim *v.* 宣告；公布

waited for me to follow. Was I in trouble? My grandfather was a highly intelligent, quiet man. He had never said a harsh word to me, and maybe this was to be the first time? Or maybe he would ask that I get back in the car and apologize to my grandmother. I had no experience in this *realm* with my grandparents and no way to *gauge* what the consequences might be. We stopped beside the trailer. My grandfather looked at me, and after a bit of silence, he gently and calmly said, "Jeff, one day you'll understand that it's harder to be kind than clever."

What I want to talk to you about today is the difference between gifts and choices. Cleverness is a gift, kindness is a choice. Gifts are easy—they're given after all. Choices can be hard. You can *seduce* yourself with your gifts if you're not careful, and if you do, it'll probably be to the *detriment* of your choices.

This is a group with many gifts. I'm sure one of your gifts is the

---

会让我回到车上跟祖母道歉？我以前从未遇到过这种状况，因而也无从知晓会有什么后果发生。我们在房车旁停下来。祖父注视着我，沉默片刻，然后轻轻地、平静地说："杰夫，有一天你会明白，善良比聪明更难。"

今天我想告诉你们的是天赋和选择的区别。聪明是一种天赋，而善良是一种选择。天赋易得——与生俱来，而选择则颇为不易。一不小心，你就有可能被天赋所诱惑，而这可能会损害到你做出的选择。

在座各位都是拥有天赋的人才。我相信你们的天赋之一就是拥有精明能干的头脑。我之所以这么认为，是因为在竞争如此激烈的入学考试中，如果你们不能表现出聪明才智，便没有资格进入这所学校。

---

realm *n.* 界；领域　　　　gauge *v.* 估计；计量
seduce *v.* 引诱；诱使　　　detriment *n.* 损害；伤害

gift of a smart and capable brain. I'm confident that's the case because admission is competitive and if there weren't some signs that you're clever, the dean of admission wouldn't have let you in.

Your smarts will come in *handy* because you will travel in a land of marvels. We humans—*plodding* as we are—will astonish ourselves. We'll invent ways to generate clean energy and a lot of it. Atom by atom, we'll assemble tiny machines that will enter cell walls and make repairs. This month comes the extraordinary but also inevitable news that we've synthesized life. In the coming years, we'll not only *synthesize* it, but we'll engineer it to specifications. I believe you'll even see us understand the human brain. Jules Verne, Mark Twain, Galileo, Newton—all the curious from the ages would have wanted to be alive most of all right now. As a civilization, we will have so many gifts, just as you as individuals have so many individual gifts as you sit before me.

你们的聪明才智必定会有用武之地，因为你们行进在一片神奇的土地上。我们人类，尽管跬步前行，却终将会令自己大吃一惊。我们能够想方设法制造清洁能源，也能够一个原子一个原子地组装微型机械，使之穿过细胞壁，修复细胞。这个月，人类终于合成了生命，这让所有人惊叹，但其出现也在常理之中。未来几年，我们不仅能合成生命，还能按说明书驱动它们。我相信有朝一日，我们甚至能理解人类的大脑。儒勒·凡尔纳、马克·吐温、伽利略、牛顿，所有这些充满好奇之心的人都希望能够活到现在。作为文明时代的产物，我们会拥有天赋奇才，正如在座的各位，每一个生命个体都拥有独特的天赋。

---

handy *adj.* 方便的；手边的   plodding *adj.* 沉重缓慢的；单调乏味的
synthesize *v.* 合成；综合

We Are What We Choose II

Remarks by Jeff Bezos, as Delivered to the Class of 2010,
Baccalaureate Princeton University

How will you use these gifts? And will you take pride in your gifts or pride in your choices?

I got the idea to start Amazon 16 years ago. I came across the fact that Web *usage* was growing at 2,300 percent per year. I'd never seen or heard of anything that grew that fast,

决定成就我们 II

杰夫·贝佐斯在普林斯顿大学2010年毕业典礼上的讲话

　　那如何让这些天赋物尽其用呢？你们是会为自己的天赋而骄傲，还是会为自己的选择而骄傲？

　　16年前，我萌生了创办亚马逊的想法。那时互联网的使用量以每年2，300%的速度增长，这是我从未看到或听过的。因此我萌生了一个想法——创建一个涵盖几百万种书籍的网上书店。这在物质世界里根本无法

usage *n.* 使用

and the idea of building an online bookstore with millions of titles—something that simply couldn't exist in the physical world—was very exciting to me. I had just turned 30 years old, and I'd been married for a year.

I told my wife MacKenzie that I wanted to quit my job and go to do this crazy thing that probably wouldn't work since most startups don't, and I wasn't sure what would happen after that. MacKenzie told me I should go for it. As a young boy, I'd been a garage inventor. I'd invented an automatic gate closer out of *cement*-filled tires, a solar cooker that didn't work very well out of an umbrella and *tinfoil*, baking-pan alarms to *entrap* my *siblings*. I'd always wanted to be an inventor, and she wanted me to follow my passion.

I was working at a financial firm in New York City with a bunch of

---

存在，但我还是为此而兴奋异常。那时我刚刚30岁，结婚才一年。

我告诉妻子麦肯思我想辞去工作，去做这件疯狂而且可能会失败的事情，因为大部分创业公司都是如此，而且我也不确定之后会发生什么。麦肯思告诉我应该去放手一搏。小时候，我就是车库发明家。我曾用水泥填充的轮胎制作了一个自动关门器、用雨伞、锡纸做了一个性能不太好的太阳能炉灶和一个恶搞我兄弟的烘焙报警器。我一直想做一个发明家，麦肯思也支持我追随内心的热情。

我当时在纽约一家金融公司工作，与一群非常聪明的人共事，我的老

---

cement *n.* 水泥；胶结材料　　　　　　　tinfoil *n.* 锡纸
entrap *v.* 使入陷阱　　　　　　　　　　sibling *n.* 兄弟或姊妹

very smart people, and I had a brilliant boss that I much admired. I went to my boss and told him I wanted to start a company selling books on the Internet. He took me on a long walk in Central Park, listened carefully to me, and finally said, "That sounds like a really good idea, but it would be an even better idea for someone who didn't already have a good job."

That logic made some sense to me, and he convinced me to think about it for 48 hours before making a final decision. Seen in that light, it really was a difficult choice, but ultimately, I decided I had to *give it a shot*. I didn't think I'd regret trying and failing. And I suspected I would always be *haunted* by a decision to not try at all. After much consideration, I took the less safe path to follow my passion, and I'm proud of that choice.

Tomorrow, in a very real sense, your life—the life you author from

---

板智慧超群，很让人崇拜。我告诉他我想开办一家在网上卖书的公司。他带我在中央公园漫步良久，认真地听我讲完后说："这个主意听起来真不错，但是对那些目前没有谋到一份好工作的人来说，这更是个好主意。"

这一逻辑对我而言颇有道理，他劝我在最终做出决定之前再考虑48小时。那样想来，这个决定确实很艰难，但是最终，我决定拼一次。尝试过后即使失败了，我也不会有遗憾，倒是决定了之后却不付诸行动会更让我备受煎熬。深思熟虑之后，我选择了那条看似不安全的道路，去追随我内心的热情。我为那个决定而感到骄傲。

明天，非常现实地说，你们即将开启从零开始塑造自己人生的时代。

---

give it a shot   试一试   haunt *v.* 使苦恼；萦绕

scratch on your own—begins.

How will you use your gifts? What choices will you make?

Will inertia be your guide, or will you follow your passions?

Will you follow *dogma*, or will you be original?

Will you choose a life of ease, or a life of service and adventure?

Will you *wilt* under criticism, or will you follow your convictions?

Will you bluff it out when you're wrong, or will you apologize?

Will you guard your heart against rejection, or will you act when you fall in love?

Will you play it safe, or will you be a little bit *swashbuckling*?

When it's tough, will you give up, or will you be *relentless*?

你们会如何运用自己的天赋?你们又会做出怎样的抉择?

你们是被惯性所引导，还是追随自己内心的热情?

你们会墨守成规，还是勇于创新?

你们会选择安逸的生活，还是选择一个奉献与冒险的人生?

你们会屈服于批评，还是会坚守信念?

你们会掩饰错误，还是会坦诚道歉?

你们在面对爱情时会因害怕拒绝而掩饰内心，还是会勇往直前?

你们想要波澜不惊，还是想要搏击风浪?

你们在严峻的现实之下会选择放弃，还是会义无反顾地前行?

---

dogma *n.* 教条

swashbuckling *adj.* 恃强凌弱的

wilt *v.* 使……凋谢；枯萎

relentless *adj.* 残酷的；不留情的

Will you be a cynic, or will you be a builder?

Will you be clever at the expense of others, or will you be kind?

I will *hazard* a prediction. When you are 80 years old, and in a quiet moment of reflection *narrating* for only yourself the most personal version of your life story, the telling that will be most compact and meaningful will be the series of choices you have made.

In the end, we are our choices. Build yourself a great story.

Thank you and good luck!

你们要做愤世嫉俗者，还是踏实的建设者？

你们要不计一切代价地展示聪明，还是选择善良？

我们预测一下：等你们到80岁追忆往昔时，只有你一个人静静对内心诉说你的人生故事，其中最为充实、最有意义的那段讲述，会被你们做出的一系列决定所填满。

最后，我想说，是选择塑造了我们的人生。请为你自己塑造一个美好的人生故事吧！

谢谢！祝你们好运！

---

hazard *v.* 尝试着做；冒……风险　　　　　narrate *v.* 讲；叙述

30

Commencement Address in Yale University
—George Walker Bush

...

That's how I've come to feel about the Yale experience—*grateful*. I studied hard, I played hard, and I made a lot of *lifelong* friends. What stays with you from college is the part of your education you hardly ever notice at the time. It's the expectations and examples around you, the ideals you

在耶鲁大学毕业典礼上的演讲
——乔治·沃克·布什

……

我很感激耶鲁大学给我提供了这么好的读书环境。读书期间，我坚持"用功读书，努力玩乐"的信念，虽然学业不是十分出色，但结交了许多让我终身受益的朋友。同学们在校时可能还没有体会到大学生活的内涵，但它会伴随你一生，因其既包含丰富的学科知识和学术氛围，又蕴涵着许

---

grateful *adj.* 感激的；感谢的　　　　　　　　lifelong *adj.* 终生的

believe in, and the friends you make.

In my time, they spoke of the "Yale man". I was really never sure what that was. But I do think that I'm a better man because of Yale. All universities, *at their best*, teach that degrees and honors are far from the *full measure of* life. Nor is that measure taken in wealth or in titles. What matters most are the standards you live by, the consideration you show others, and the way you use the gifts you are given.

Now you leave Yale behind, carrying the written proof of your success here, at a college older than America. When I left here, I didn't have much in the way of a life plan. I knew some people who thought they did. But it turned out that we were all in for *ups and downs*, most of them unexpected. Life takes its own turns, makes its

多人生理念，还有许多值得结交的朋友。

我上大学时，大家常说"耶鲁人"，当时我并不明白那是什么意思。但是我知道，因为耶鲁，因为有了在耶鲁深造的经历，我成了一个更加优秀的人！所有一流的大学都会教会大家学位和荣耀并非生活的全部，也不是通向财富与权力的必经之路。相反，更重要的是你的人生准则，是你对他人的体谅，及你如何运用你的天赋。

现在，你们即将离开耶鲁，离开这所历史比美国还要悠久的大学，带走的是对你们在耶鲁所获成就的书面证明。我离开耶鲁时，并没有明确的人生计划。我知道有些人认为他们有，但后来发生的事情往往是我们都在经历沉沉浮浮，而大部分都不是我们所曾预料到的。人生有她自己的运行

at one's best　处于最好状态　　　full measure of　完整的；充分的
ups and downs　起伏；盛衰；成败

own demands, writes its own story. And along the way, we start to realize we are not the author.

We begin to understand that life is ours to live, but not to waste, and that the greatest rewards are found in the commitments we make with our whole hearts— to the people we love and to the causes that earn our *sacrifice*. I hope that each of you will know these rewards. I hope you will find them in your own way and your own time.

For some, that might mean some time in public service. And if you hear that calling, I hope you answer. Each of you has unique gifts and you were given them for a reason. Use them and share them. Public service is one way—an honorable way—to mark your life with meaning.

轨迹，自己的抉择，也书写着她自己的故事。我们一路走来，才开始渐渐明白，其实我们都不是这个故事的作者。

我们开始明白人生是要让我们去生活，而不是用来浪费。我们最大的收获源于对我们所爱的人，对值得为之牺牲的事业而做出的全心全意的承诺。我希望你们每个人都能了解到这些，都能以你们自己的方式在你们自己的生活中发现它们。

对于一些人来说，这可能意味着服务于公众。如果你听到这样的召唤，我希望你能做出回应。你们每一个人都有自己独特的天赋，上帝把它赐予你自有他的理由。好好利用这些天赋，并与他人分享。服务大众是一种方式——一种可敬的方式——可以让你的人生变得更有意义。

---

sacrifice *n.* 牺牲；舍身

Today I visit not only my *alma mater*, but the city of my birth. My life began just a few blocks from here, but I was raised in West Texas. From there, Yale always seemed a world away, maybe a part of my future. Now it's part of my past, and Yale for me is a source of great pride.

I hope that there will come a time for you to return to Yale to say that, and feel as I do today. And I hope you won't wait as long. Congratulations and God bless.

今天我所回到的不仅仅是我的母校，还是我出生的城市。我出生的地方离这里仅仅几个街区远，但在西德克萨斯州长大。那时，耶鲁与我仿佛隔了一个世界之遥，也许，她会是我未来的一部分，但现在，她已经成为我过去的一部分。对我而言，耶鲁是知识的源泉，也是令我极度骄傲的源泉。

我希望，将来当你们以另外一种身份回到耶鲁时，能有与我一样的感受并说出相似的话。我希望你们离耶鲁邀请你们回校演讲的日子不会太久。祝贺大家！上帝保佑你们！

alma mater　　母校；校歌